COLLECTIONS

A Harcourt Reading Program

Something new waits
for you in each story
in this book.

SOMETHING NEW

Harcourt

Orlando   Boston   Dallas   Chicago   San Diego

COLLECTIONS

A Harcourt Reading Program

SOMETHING NEW

SENIOR AUTHORS

Roger C. Farr • Dorothy S. Strickland • Isabel L. Beck

AUTHORS

Richard F. Abrahamson • Alma Flor Ada • Bernice E. Cullinan • Margaret McKeown • Nancy Roser
Patricia Smith • Judy Wallis • Junko Yokota • Hallie Kay Yopp

SENIOR CONSULTANT

Asa G. Hilliard III

CONSULTANTS

Karen S. Kutiper • David A. Monti • Angelina Olivares

Harcourt

Orlando   Boston   Dallas   Chicago   San Diego

Visit *The Learning Site!*
www.harcourtschool.com

SOMETHING NEW

Dear Reader,

Would you like something new—a new friend, a new toy, or a new idea?

In **Something New**, you will find all kinds of new things. You will read about a new girl at school who helps a boy make friends. You will meet a man who wants to make his new toy plane fly. You will learn what makes a new day.

We hope you will like every story. You are sure to find something new in each!

Sincerely,

The Authors

The Authors

THEME

Being Me

CONTENTS

Helping Hands

4

CONTENTS

CONTENTS

THEME
Our World

7

Using Reading Strategies

A strategy is a plan for doing something well.
You can use strategies when you read to help you understand a story better. First, **look at the title and pictures.** Then, **think about what you want to find out.** Using strategies like these can help you become a better reader.

Look at the list of strategies on page 9. You will learn how to use these strategies as you read the stories in this book. As you read, look back at the list to remind yourself of the **strategies good readers use.**

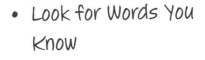

- Look for Words You Know

- Look at Word Bits and Parts

- Self-Correct

- Read Ahead

- Reread Aloud

- Use Picture Clues to Confirm Meaning

- Make and Confirm Predictions

- Sequence Events/Summarize

- Create Mental Images

- Use Context to Confirm Meaning

- Reread

- Make Inferences

Here are some ways to make sure you understand what you are reading:

✔ Copy the list of strategies onto a piece of construction paper.

✔ Fold it and use it as a bookmark as you read.

✔ After you read, talk with a classmate about the strategies you used.

THEME
Being Me

CONTENTS

Reader's Choice

Who's Who in My Family?
by Loreen Leedy
NONFICTION

The students in Ms. Fox's class learn how their family members are related to them.

Award-Winning Author
READER'S CHOICE LIBRARY

For Pete's Sake
by Ellen Stoll Walsh
FICTION

Pete, a young alligator, worries when he notices he is different from his friends.

Award-Winning Author
READER'S CHOICE LIBRARY

Beezy at Bat
by Megan McDonald
REALISTIC FICTION

Beezy and her friends find excitement around every corner.

Award-Winning Author

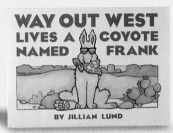

Way Out West Lives a Coyote Named Frank
by Jillian Lund
FICTION

Frank the coyote spends time with friends and alone in his desert home.

Children's Choice

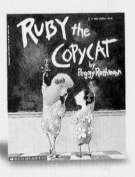

Ruby the Copycat
by Peggy Rathmann
REALISTIC FICTION

Ruby copies Angela until her teacher helps her discover her own talents.

Children's Choice

Lucy's Quiet Book

by Angela Shelf Medearis
pictures by Lisa Campbell Ernst

15

Lucy had six brothers.
They were all very loud.
Sometimes they yelled.
Sometimes they cried.
Sometimes they laughed
really loud.

16

Lucy was very quiet.

She got angry, but she never yelled.

She felt sad, but she never cried.

And she never, ever laughed
really loud.

17

When Lucy's house got too loud, she went to the library. The library was quiet. Lucy liked to help Mrs. Stone, the children's librarian. "How is my helper today?" Mrs. Stone always asked.
Lucy just smiled.

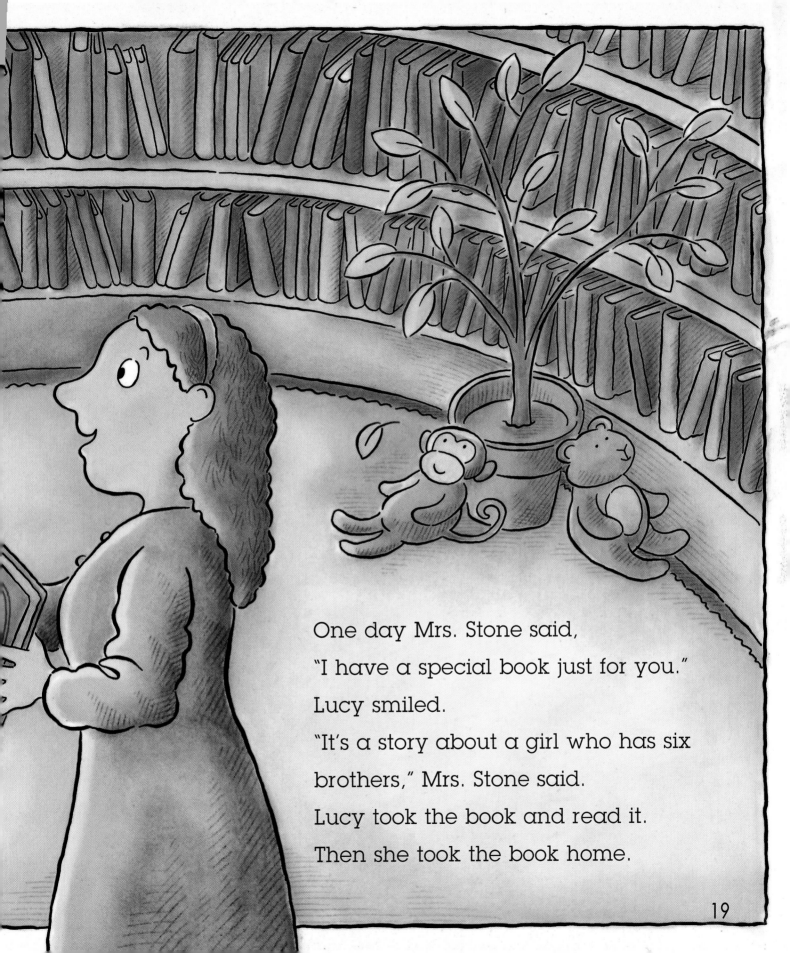

One day Mrs. Stone said,

"I have a special book just for you."

Lucy smiled.

"It's a story about a girl who has six

brothers," Mrs. Stone said.

Lucy took the book and read it.

Then she took the book home.

19

Timmy and Tommy were yelling.
Billy and Bobby were crying.
Sid and Sammy were laughing
really loud.
The house was very, very, very noisy!
Lucy had an idea.

21

Suddenly, Timmy, Tommy, Billy,
Bobby, Sid, and Sammy were quiet.
They couldn't believe their ears!
Lucy could be as loud as they were.
Lucy surprised herself most of all.
She grinned and began to read.

The next day, Lucy took the book back to the library. When she got there, she couldn't believe her ears.

Children were yelling.

Children were crying.

Children were laughing
really loud.

Lucy knew just what to do.

24

25

Suddenly the library was quiet.

Then Lucy began to read.

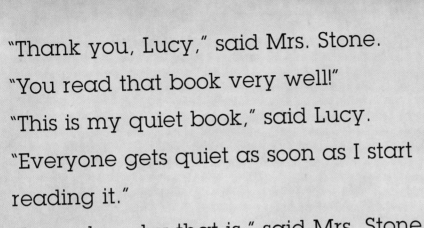

"Thank you, Lucy," said Mrs. Stone.
"You read that book very well!"
"This is my quiet book," said Lucy.
"Everyone gets quiet as soon as I start reading it."
"I wonder why that is," said Mrs. Stone.

Lucy just smiled.

Think About It

1. What makes Lucy's brothers and the children at the library become quiet?

2. What do you like most about this story?

3. How do the author and illustrator show that Lucy changes during the story?

Meet the Author and the Illustrator

Angela Shelf Medearis

Q: How is Lucy like you?

A: Lucy loves to read and loves going to the library, just like me!

Angela Shelf Medearis

Lisa Campbell Ernst

Q: How is Lucy like you?

A: Like Lucy, I love going to the library! It is a place that has surprises on every shelf.

Lisa Campbell Ernst

Visit *The Learning Site!*
www.harcourtschool.com

29

Pages

The pages in a book
Sit glued and bound.
I turn the pages,
And they turn me around.

by Douglas Florian
illustrated by Holly Cooper

31

RESPONSE

BOOKS, BOOKS, BOOKS!

Create a book jacket

Lucy finds a book that she likes to read. Do you have some favorite books that you like to read?

Make a cover for one of your favorite books. On a sheet of paper, draw a picture for your book cover. Write the title of your book on your paper. Then, finish this sentence and write it below your picture:

This is a good book to read because _____.

Share your book cover with classmates.

Amelia Bedelia is a good book because it makes me laugh.

ACTIVITY

RULES TO READ BY Write a list

In "Lucy's Quiet Book," the children in the library make a lot of noise. Work with a partner to make a sign of library rules. Write three rules. Try to make your sign look fun and friendly.

Hang your sign near your classroom library.

Library Rules
★ Please talk softly.
Be kind to books.

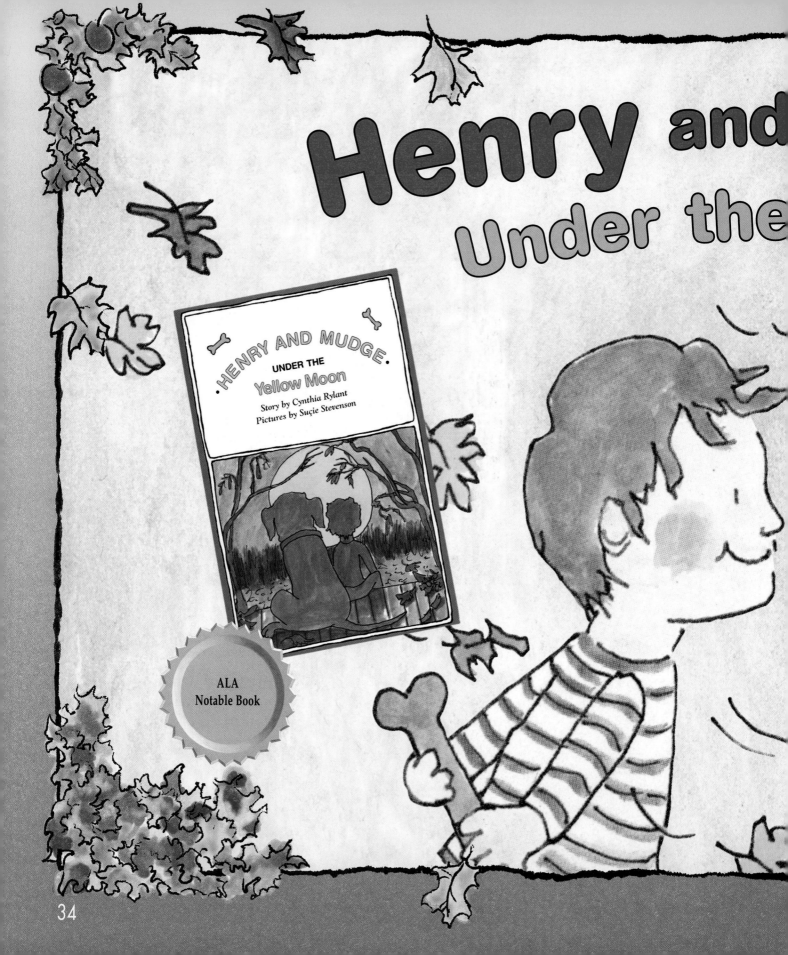

Henry and
Under the

HENRY AND MUDGE.
UNDER THE
Yellow Moon
Story by Cynthia Rylant
Pictures by Suçie Stevenson

ALA
Notable Book

Mudge
Yellow Moon

Story by Cynthia Rylant
Pictures by Suçie Stevenson

Together in the Fall

In the fall,
Henry and his big dog Mudge
took long walks in the woods.

Henry loved looking at
the tops of the trees.
He liked the leaves:
orange, yellow, brown, and red.

Mudge loved sniffing at the ground.

And he liked the leaves, too.

He always ate a few.

In the fall,
Henry liked counting the birds
flying south.
Mudge liked
watching for busy chipmunks.

Since one was a boy
and the other was a dog,
they never did things
just the same way.

Henry picked apples
and Mudge licked apples.

Henry put on a coat
and Mudge grew one.
And when the fall wind blew,
Henry's ears turned red
and Mudge's ears
turned inside out.

But one thing about them
was the same.
In the fall
Henry and Mudge liked
being together,
most of all.

Think About It

1. What do Henry and Mudge like to do together in the fall?

2. What do you like to do in the fall?

3. Do you think Henry and Mudge will have this much fun in the winter, spring, and summer? Explain your answer.

Meet the Author
Cynthia Rylant

Dear Readers,

I have two dogs named Martha Jane and Gracie Rose. Martha Jane is a big, white dog. She loves to eat pizza, chase tennis balls, and sleep on the couch. Gracie Rose is a little, short-legged dog. She loves to howl. I like to walk with my dogs just as Henry likes to go for walks with Mudge.

Cynthia Rylant

Visit *The Learning Site!*
www.harcourtschool.com

Meet the Illustrator
Suçie Stevenson

Dear Readers,

I love drawing the pictures in the Henry and Mudge books. I have a new puppy named Merlin. He is an English mastiff dog, just like Mudge. Merlin is a lovely pup who drools only a little. When he is big, he will weigh 240 pounds and drool a lot!

Suçie Stevenson

Response Activities

How-To Pet Care Make a book

Henry must take good care of Mudge. Work with a partner to write a pet care book.

1. Pick a pet that you would like to care for.

2. Read about your pet in books about pets or in an encyclopedia CD-ROM.

3. On half sheets of paper, write steps for caring for your pet.

4. Draw pictures for your pages.

5. Make a cover. Write a title for your book.

Feed your cat.

Staple your pages and cover together. Add your book to a class pet care library.

Fall Scenes Make a collage

Henry and Mudge like to do many things in the fall. What do you like to do in the fall? You can make a collage of a fall scene.

You will need:

magazines
to cut up

leaves

construction
paper

scissors

glue

1. Think of a fall scene for your collage.

2. Cut pictures out of magazines to show your scene.

3. Glue the pictures onto a big sheet of paper.

4. Add leaves or cut leaf shapes from red, yellow, and orange construction paper.

Share your collage with classmates.

Setting

In "Henry and Mudge Under the Yellow Moon," you read about things that Henry and Mudge do together. When and where do they do those things? The time and place a story happens is the **setting**. The pictures and words in a story help you understand the setting.

The setting of "Henry and Mudge Under the Yellow Moon" is the woods in the fall. The story web below shows some of the things that help you understand this setting.

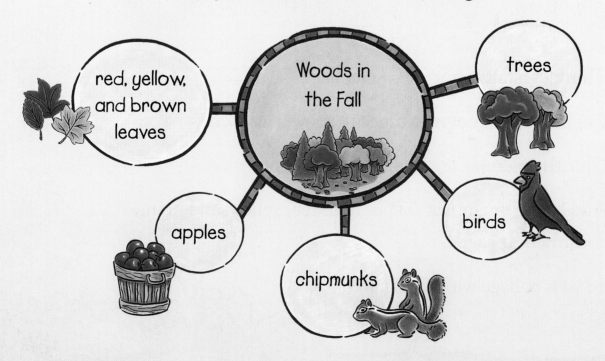

red, yellow, and brown leaves

Woods in the Fall

trees

apples

chipmunks

birds

When you know the setting of a story, you can understand the story better. As you read, think about when and where a story happens. Look for clues in the pictures and the words to figure out what the setting is.

1 Imagine that you are reading a story about a horse running to a barn through the snow. What do you think the setting of the story is?

2 Imagine that you are writing a story about riding in a car. What clues would you give to help readers understand the setting?

Visit *The Learning Site!*
www.harcourtschool.com

Plan a story that takes place in your classroom. Think of clues that make the setting of your story clear. Draw a web like the one below. Write a clue in each circle.

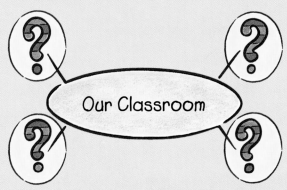

Our Classroom

49

Days With

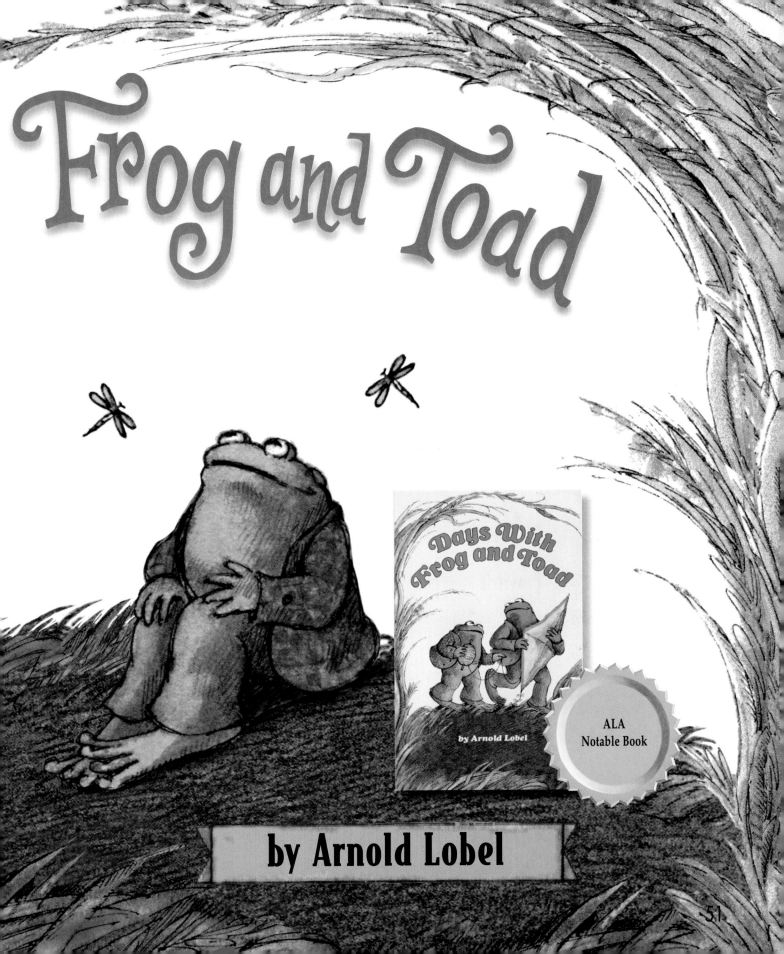

Frog and Toad

by Arnold Lobel

Days With Frog and Toad

by Arnold Lobel

ALA
Notable Book

Alone

Toad went to Frog's house.

He found a note on the door.

The note said,

"Dear Toad, I am not at home.

I went out.

I want to be alone."

"Alone?" said Toad.

"Frog has me for a friend.

Why does he want to be alone?"

Toad looked through the windows.

He looked in the garden.

He did not see Frog.

Toad went to the woods.

Frog was not there.

He went to the meadow.

Frog was not there.

Toad went down to the river.

There was Frog.

He was sitting on an island

by himself.

"Poor Frog," said Toad.

"He must be very sad.

I will cheer him up."

Toad ran home.

He made sandwiches.

He made a pitcher of iced tea.

He put everything

in a basket.

Toad hurried

back to the river.

"Frog," he shouted,

"it's me.

It's your best friend, Toad!"

Frog was too far away to hear.

Toad took off his jacket

and waved it like a flag.

Frog was too far away to see.

Toad shouted and waved,

but it was no use.

Frog sat on the island.

He did not see or hear Toad.

A turtle swam by.

Toad climbed on the turtle's back.

"Turtle," said Toad,

"carry me to the island.

Frog is there.

He wants to be alone."

"If Frog wants to be alone,"

said the turtle,

"why don't you leave him alone?"

"Maybe you are right," said Toad.

"Maybe Frog does not

want to see me.

Maybe he does not want me

to be his friend anymore."

"Yes, maybe," said the turtle

as he swam to the island.

"Frog!" cried Toad.

"I am sorry for all

the dumb things I do.

I am sorry for all

the silly things I say.

Please be my friend again!"

Toad slipped off the turtle.

With a splash, he fell in the river.

Frog pulled Toad

up onto the island.

Toad looked in the basket.

The sandwiches were wet.

The pitcher of iced tea was empty.

"Our lunch is spoiled," said Toad.

"I made it for you, Frog,

so that you would be happy."

"But Toad," said Frog.

"I *am* happy. I am very happy.

This morning

when I woke up

I felt good because

the sun was shining.

I felt good because

I was a frog.

And I felt good because

I have you for a friend.

I wanted to be alone.

I wanted to think about

how fine everything is."

"Oh," said Toad.

"I guess that is a very good reason

for wanting to be alone."

"Now," said Frog,

"I will be glad *not* to be alone.

Let's eat lunch."

Frog and Toad

stayed on the island

all afternoon.

They ate wet sandwiches

without iced tea.

They were two close friends

sitting alone together.

Think About It

1 Why was Frog sitting by himself?

2 Do you like to be alone sometimes?
What do you like to think about when
you are alone?

3 Why did Toad try to cheer up Frog?

About the Author and Illustrator
Arnold Lobel

Arnold Lobel's children used to catch frogs and toads in the summertime. The toads made great pets. The Lobels put them in an aquarium, fed them, and gave them milk baths. Because Arnold Lobel was so interested in these animals, he wrote many stories about Frog and Toad.

Visit *The Learning Site!*
www.harcourtschool.com

65

Sometimes

Sometimes I like to be alone
And look up at the sky
And think my thoughts inside my head—
Just me, myself, and I.

by Mary Ann Hoberman

illustrated by Steve Johnson and Lou Fancher

Response Activities

Friendship Song

Make up a song

Make up a class song about friendship.

1. Sit in a circle.

2. Make up a rhythm for your song. Clap your hands and tap your feet.

3. Now say these words to your rhythm: A friend is someone who _____.

4. Go around the circle. Everybody claps and taps the rhythm while each person adds one thing about a friend.

Try not to miss a beat!

Let's Get Together!

Make a card

Frog and Toad often like being together. Think of a person or a pet you like to spend time with. Make a card to give to that person or pet.

1. Fold a sheet of paper in half.

2. On the outside of the folded paper, draw the front of your card.

3. Open the card and write a note to your friend. Write your name under the note.

Let's ride our bikes after school!
Tom

Wilson Sat

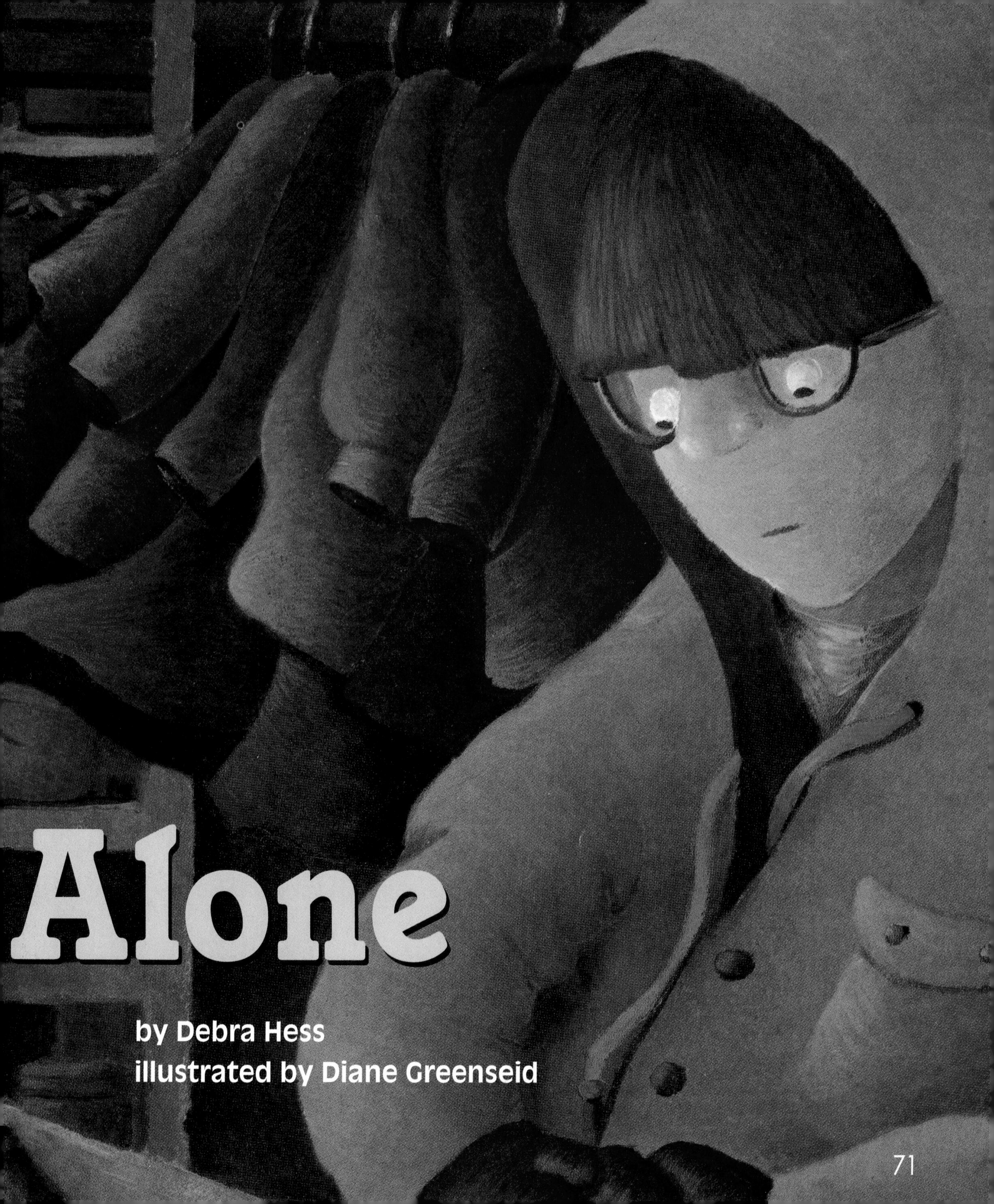

Alone

by Debra Hess

illustrated by Diane Greenseid

On Mondays the children in Ms. Caraway's
class pushed their desks together and sat in
groups of six and seven.

Wilson sat alone.

At lunchtime,
when groups of
friends ate together
in the cafeteria,

Wilson ate alone.

75

At recess, when everyone
gathered for a kick ball game,
or played Cowboys and Indians,
or Dinosaurs and Monsters,

Wilson played alone.

And at the end of the day, when all the children rode the bus, or climbed into cars, or wandered home in packs of three or four . . .

Wilson walked alone.

On reading days, while everyone clustered into groups,

Wilson read alone.

On snow days, as Ben and Sam and Lucy and Meg
helped each other into their snowsuits,

Wilson dressed alone.

When the children built snowmen, and
threw snow, and laughed and screamed,
Wilson didn't laugh . . .

because he was alone.

One day a new girl came to school.
She said her name was Sara.
She smiled all the time.

She sat alone, and ate alone,
and read alone, and played alone.

But only for one day.

On her second day at school, Sara pushed
her desk into a group of other desks,
and ate with the other children,
and played Monsters in the snow,
and laughed.

And Wilson watched her from
where he sat,
alone.
He watched her all that day,
and all the next day, too.

And Sara saw him watching,
and raced across the snow,

and roared a monster roar at Wilson,
who sat alone.

83

"Don't do that!" said Lucy.

"Not to Wilson," called Sam.

"Why not?" asked Sara.

"He always sits alone," said Sam.

"He always plays alone," said Meg.

"He likes to be alone," said Ben.

And then

an amazing thing happened.

Wilson roared back.

Softly at first, and then louder,
and louder, and louder. . . .

It was the biggest, loudest,
grandest monster roar of all time.

And from that day on,
Wilson played with the other
children, and ate with them,
and sat with them, and read
with them, and walked
with them.

87

And Wilson was not alone anymore.

Think About It

1 How does Wilson change from the beginning of the story to the end?

2 Would you like to have a friend like Sara? Why or why not?

3 Why did Wilson roar back?

Meet the Author and the Illustrator

Debra Hess

Debra Hess says that she almost never sat alone when she was a young girl. She talked to everyone just as Sara does.

Debra Hess lives in New York with her husband. She is the author of many plays and books for children.

Diane Greenseid

Diane Greenseid has illustrated many magazines and newsletters. This is the first time she has illustrated a children's book. She is known for using beautiful colors in her pictures.

Diane Greenseid lives in California.

Visit *The Learning Site!*
www.harcourtschool.com

89

Response Activities

All Smiles Follow a recipe

Make a smile you can eat! When Sara comes to school, she smiles all the time. You and your friends can share a treat that will make you smile, too.

You will need:

- 1 red apple cut into 8 slices
- peanut butter • tiny marshmallows
- plastic knife • napkins

1. Spread peanut butter on one side of an apple slice.
2. Push marshmallows into the peanut butter.
3. Spread peanut butter on another apple slice. Then put it on top to finish the smile.
4. Share your treat with friends. Tell them how you made it.

I have a surprise for you!

Surprise!

Write a class book

At the end of the story, Wilson and Sara like doing things together. What do you think they might do to surprise each other?

1. Work with a partner. One of you can be Sara and the other can be Wilson.

2. Plan a surprise for the other character. Draw and write about it.

3. Give hints to help your partner guess the surprise.

4. Show it to your partner. Make a class book with everyone's pages.

Characters' Feelings and Actions

Story characters have feelings, just like you. You can tell how a story character feels by reading what the character says and does. Think about how you would feel if you were that character.

At the beginning of "Wilson Sat Alone," you read that Wilson does everything alone. He does not talk or play with the other children. You can see that Wilson is not smiling. How do you think he feels?

The sentences in this chart are clues that tell you about Wilson's feelings.

At the Beginning	At the End
Wilson plays alone.	Wilson plays with others.
Wilson does not laugh.	Wilson laughs.
Wilson is not smiling.	Wilson smiles.

You can tell that Wilson feels sad and lonely at the beginning of the story. How does Wilson feel at the end? Wilson plays with others and laughs and smiles. He must be feeling happy.

As you read, think about what a character in a story does and says and what a character looks like. Ask yourself, "How would I feel if I were the character?" This will help you figure out how a character feels.

WHAT HAVE YOU LEARNED?

Reread pages 86 and 87 of "Wilson Sat Alone." Look at the picture.

1. What does Wilson do on these pages? What does he look like?

2. How does Wilson feel at this point in the story?

Visit *The Learning Site!*
www.harcourtschool.com

TRY THIS • TRY THIS • TRY THIS

Look back at another story that you have read. Choose a character in that story. How does the character feel? How do you know?

On a sheet of paper, write what your character does, says, and looks like. Trade papers with a partner. Have your partner read your clues and write a sentence telling how your character feels.

94

The Mixed-Up Chameleon

by Eric Carle

Award-Winning
Author/Illustrator

On a shiny green leaf sat a small green chameleon.
It moved onto a brown tree and turned brownish.
Then it rested on a red flower and turned reddish.
When the chameleon moved slowly across the yellow
sand, it turned yellowish. You could hardly see it.

When the chameleon
was warm and had
something to eat, it
turned sparkling green.

But when it was cold and hungry,
it turned gray and dull.

When the chameleon was hungry,
it sat still and waited.
Only its eyes moved—up, down, sideways—
until it spotted a fly.
Then the chameleon's long and sticky tongue
shot out and caught the fly.
That was its life.
It was not very exciting.
But one day...

... the chameleon saw a zoo!
It had never seen so many beautiful animals.

ZOO

The chameleon thought:
How small I am, how slow, how weak!
I wish I could be big and white like a polar bear.
And the chameleon's wish came true.
But was it happy?
No!

103

I wish I could be handsome like a flamingo.

104

I wish I could be smart like a fox.

106

I wish I could swim like a fish.

109

I wish I could run like a deer.

111

I wish I could see things far away like a giraffe.

113

I wish I could hide in a shell like a turtle.

115

I wish I could be strong like an elephant.

117

I wish I could be funny like a seal.

118

119

*I wish I could be
like people.*
Just then a fly flew by.
The chameleon was very hungry.
But the chameleon was very mixed-up.
It was a little of this and it was a little of that.
And it couldn't catch the fly.

120

I wish I could be myself.
The chameleon's wish came true.
And it caught the fly!

Think About It

1. What are the animals that the chameleon wants to be like, and why does it want to be like them?

2. What does it mean to "be yourself"?

3. Why did Eric Carle title his book *The Mixed-Up Chameleon*?

Meet the Author and Illustrator

Dear Readers,

I got the idea for *The Mixed-Up Chameleon* by talking to children just like you. When I visited schools, I asked children to tell me their favorite animals. On a large sheet of paper, I drew the most important part of each animal, such as a fox's tail, an elephant's trunk, and a giraffe's neck. These pictures gave me the idea for this story. I hope you had fun reading it.

Best wishes,

Visit *The Learning Site!*
www.harcourtschool.com

Fun Animal Facts: Cham

To hide from its enemies, a chameleon changes colors. If you could do that, you'd never need new clothes!

eleons

Chameleons have tongues that are longer than their bodies. They whip them out to zap their food!

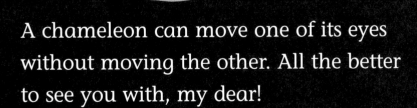

A chameleon can move one of its eyes without moving the other. All the better to see you with, my dear!

Think About It

How is the chameleon a special animal?

Response

Special Animals
Make a chart

The chameleon thinks each zoo animal is special. Work with a group to make a chart. List the nine animals the chameleon sees. Then list what he thinks is special about each animal on a sheet of paper.

Think of three more animals. What makes each one special?
Add the animals and what makes them special to your chart.

Animal	What makes it special
polar bear	big
flamingo	handsome
fox	
fish	
deer	
giraffe	
turtle	
elephant	
seal	

Activities

Mixed-Up Animals! Make a picture

When the chameleon becomes mixed-up, it looks funny.
Make a picture of another mixed-up animal.

1. Cut pictures of animals out of old magazines.

2. Decide how you will mix up the animal parts.

3. Cut out the parts you will use, and glue them together
   to make one mixed-up animal.

4. Give your animal a name. Write about
   your mixed-up animal.

Share your mixed-up
animal with
classmates.

Theme Wrap-Up

Picture This!

DRAW A PICTURE   Choose a story from
this theme. Draw a picture that shows
your favorite part. Share your picture
with your classmates. Tell why the part
you chose to draw was your favorite.

Favorite Stories

DISCUSS THE LITERATURE   Get together
with a few classmates. Talk about the
stories in this theme. Tell which story is
your favorite and why.

Prints Here, Prints There

WRITE ABOUT CHARACTER TRAITS
Handprints, paw prints, and the footprints of a chameleon are all reminders of characters in this theme. Draw a large print made by a character in this theme. Inside it, write words that tell about your character. Share your print and tell why you chose the character.

Helping Hands

CONTENTS

133

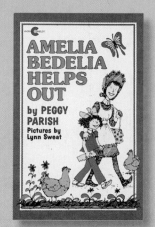

Amelia Bedelia Helps Out
by Peggy Parish

REALISTIC FICTION

When Amelia Bedelia and her niece help out Miss Emma, anything can happen!

Award-Winning Author
READER'S CHOICE LIBRARY

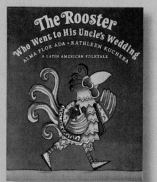

The Rooster Who Went to His Uncle's Wedding
by Alma Flor Ada

LATIN AMERICAN FOLKTALE

A rooster needs his beak cleaned, but he can't find anyone who will help him.

Award-Winning Author
READER'S CHOICE LIBRARY

Puddle Jumper: How a Toy Is Made
by Ann Morris

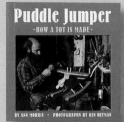

NONFICTION

Sarah helps her dad make a puddle jumper. What is it? How is it made? You'll soon find out!

Award-Winning Author

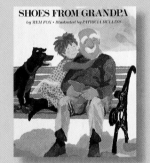

Shoes from Grandpa
by Mem Fox

CUMULATIVE TALE

Jessie's family tells her about the clothes they will give her to go with the shoes from her grandfather.

Award-Winning Author
Award-Winning Illustrator

One Duck Stuck
by Phyllis Root

FICTION

Different animals try to help a duck that is stuck in the sleepy, slimy marsh.

Award-Winning Author

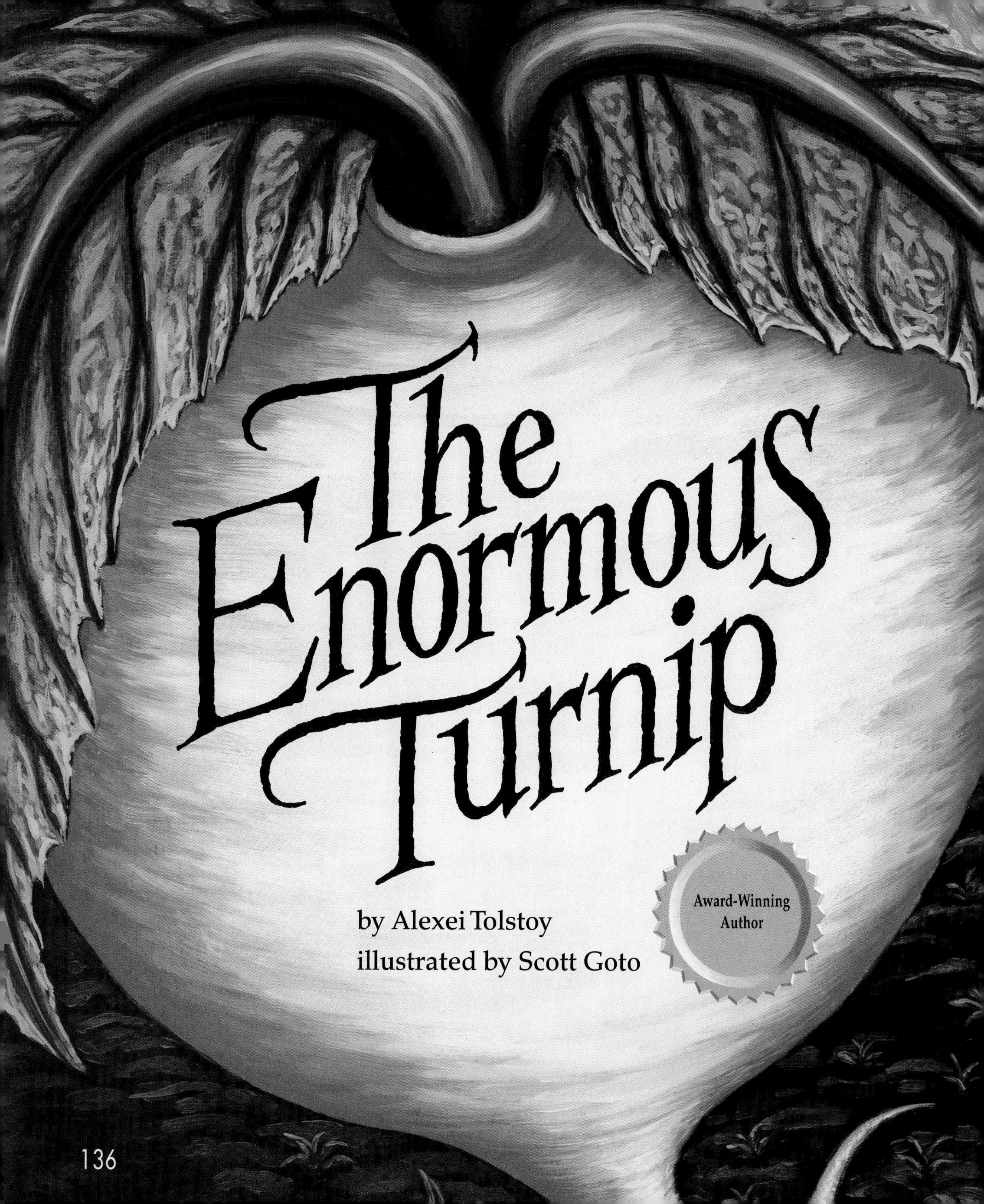

The Enormous Turnip

by Alexei Tolstoy

illustrated by Scott Goto

Award-Winning Author

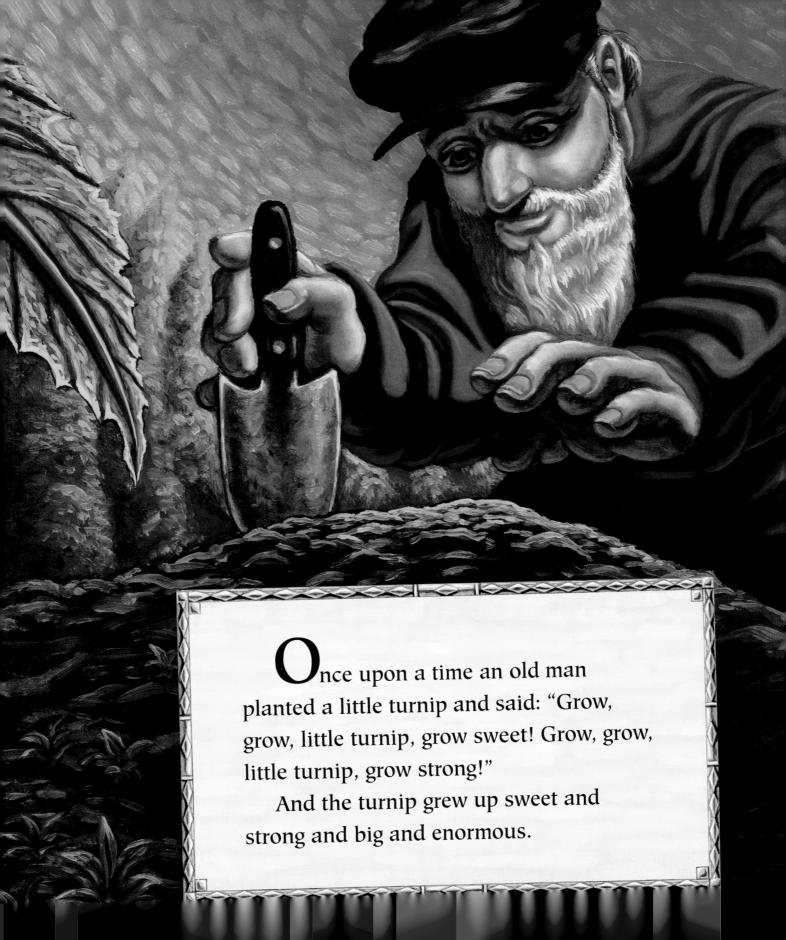

Once upon a time an old man planted a little turnip and said: "Grow, grow, little turnip, grow sweet! Grow, grow, little turnip, grow strong!"

And the turnip grew up sweet and strong and big and enormous.

Then, one day, the old man went to pull it up. He pulled and pulled again, but he could not pull it up.

He called the old woman.
The old woman pulled the old man,
The old man pulled the turnip.
    And they pulled and pulled again,
but they could not pull it up.

140

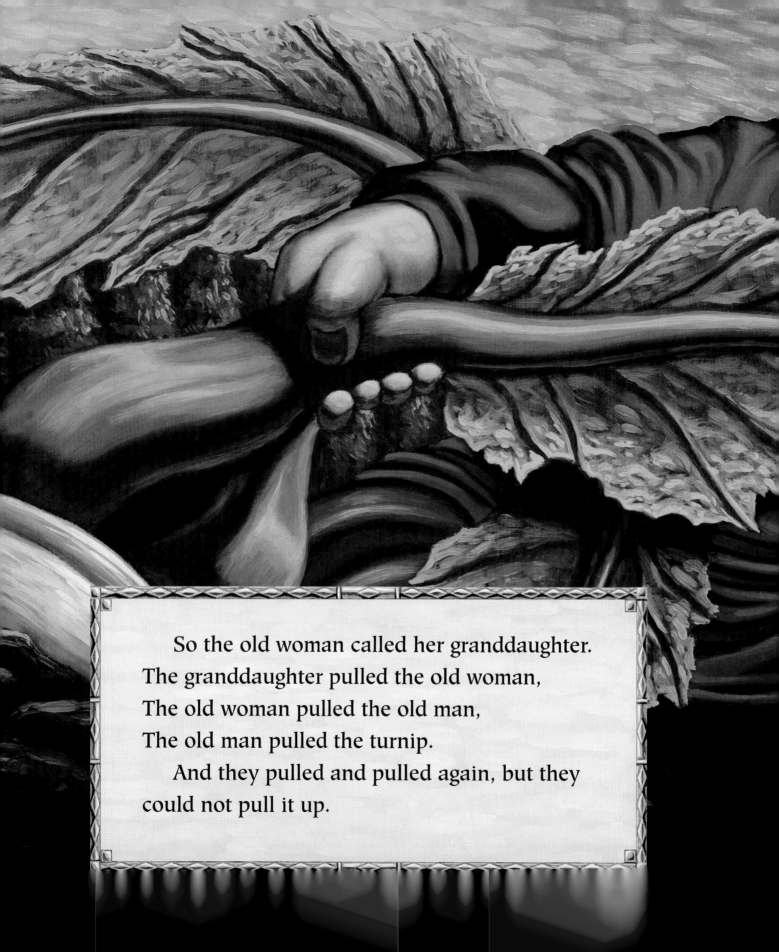

So the old woman called her granddaughter.
The granddaughter pulled the old woman,
The old woman pulled the old man,
The old man pulled the turnip.

And they pulled and pulled again, but they
could not pull it up.

The granddaughter called the black dog.
The black dog pulled the granddaughter,
The granddaughter pulled the old woman,
The old woman pulled the old man,
The old man pulled the turnip.

And they pulled and pulled again, but they could not pull it up.

144

The black dog called the cat.
The cat pulled the dog,
The dog pulled the granddaughter,
The granddaughter pulled the old woman,
The old woman pulled the old man,
The old man pulled the turnip.
    And they pulled and pulled again, but still they could not pull it up.

The cat called the mouse.
The mouse pulled the cat,
The cat pulled the dog,
The dog pulled the granddaughter,
The granddaughter pulled the old woman,
The old woman pulled the old man,
The old man pulled the turnip.
And they pulled and pulled again,

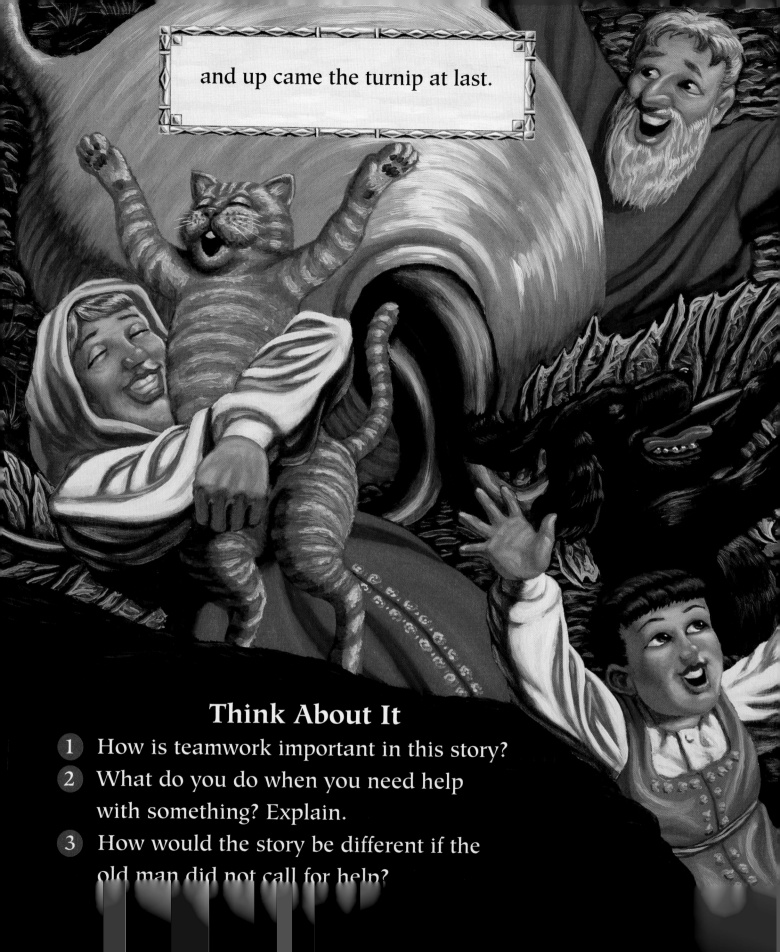

and up came the turnip at last.

Think About It

1. How is teamwork important in this story?
2. What do you do when you need help with something? Explain.
3. How would the story be different if the old man did not call for help?

About the Author

ALEXEI TOLSTOY was a popular writer in Russia. He wrote children's tales, poems, plays, and long stories. He also liked to write science-fiction stories. One of his stories is about people going to the planet Mars.

Meet the Illustrator

SCOTT GOTO has been drawing since he was a child. His love of art makes him work very hard to be the best artist he can be. He loves listening to music, playing the guitar, and watching cartoons. Scott Goto also loves learning about history.

 Visit *The Learning Site!*
www.harcourtschool.com

149

Response Activities

Help Is on the Way! Write a story

You can write a story like "The Enormous Turnip."

1. Choose a vegetable or fruit.

2. Choose five characters that will help each other.

3. Use your imagination to write a story about characters who work together to pull up or pick the vegetable or fruit.

4. Illustrate your story.

Share your story with classmates.

Can You Remember? Play a memory game

In the story, several characters help pull up the turnip. Test your memory as you add new characters in this game.

1. Sit in a circle.

2. The first person says, "**I pulled up the turnip with help from a _____,**" and name something, such as **dog**.

3. The next person repeats what was said and adds another thing. That person might say, "**I pulled up the turnip with help from a dog and a cat.**"

See how long your group's list can get!

Sequence

A story is made up of many story events. These are the things that happen in a story. When authors write stories, they often start with what happens first. Then they write about the other story events in the order, or sequence, in which they happen. The last story event is at the end of the story.

Think about the story events in "The Enormous Turnip." What happens first? What is the next thing that happens?

The sentences in the chart show the first three story events in "The Enormous Turnip."

An old man plants a turnip.

↓

The turnip grows big.

↓

The old man cannot pull it up.

The **first** thing that happens is an old man plants a turnip. The **next** thing that happens is the turnip grows big. **Then** what happens?

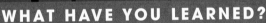

Look for time words such as *first, next, then,* and *last* to help you understand the order of story events. When you know the order in which things happen, you understand a story better.

WHAT HAVE YOU LEARNED?

1. What happens after the old man and old woman cannot pull up the turnip?

2. Reread pages 147 and 148 of "The Enormous Turnip." What time word do you find? How does it help you understand the story's order?

Visit *The Learning Site!*
www.harcourtschool.com

TRY THIS • TRY THIS • TRY THIS

Look back at another story that you have read. Choose three story events. Write a sentence about each event in story order. Draw boxes and arrows to show which story event happens first, next, and last.

Helping
Out

Words and photographs by George Ancona

Award-
Winning Author/
Photographer

Helping Out

Words and

photographs by

George Ancona

Helping out can be as
simple as being there to
hand someone a tool
when he needs it.

In early spring, you can help to plant seeds in the vegetable garden. Soon they will sprout and grow into many good things to eat.

You can turn some chores into fun, like washing the car on a hot summer's day.

Some jobs can be dirty, like changing the oil in the engine of a car.

At school, a teacher needs
help keeping the classroom
neat and clean.

When you work alongside
an adult and do a good job,
you feel pretty big.

162

After you learn to do things well, you can begin to get paid for your work.

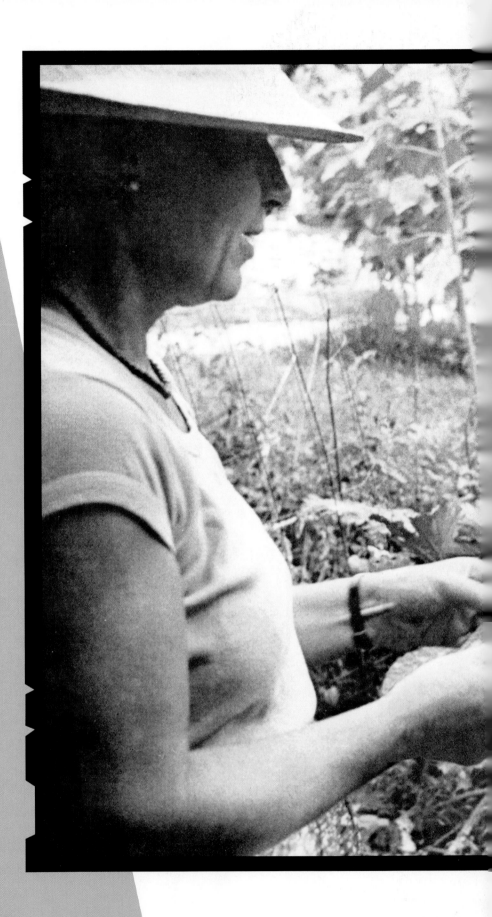

But the best thing about helping out is that it can bring two people closer together.

Think About It

1 How do the children in this book help others?

2 What are some things you can do to help out at school?

3 Would this book be as interesting without photographs? Why or why not?

166

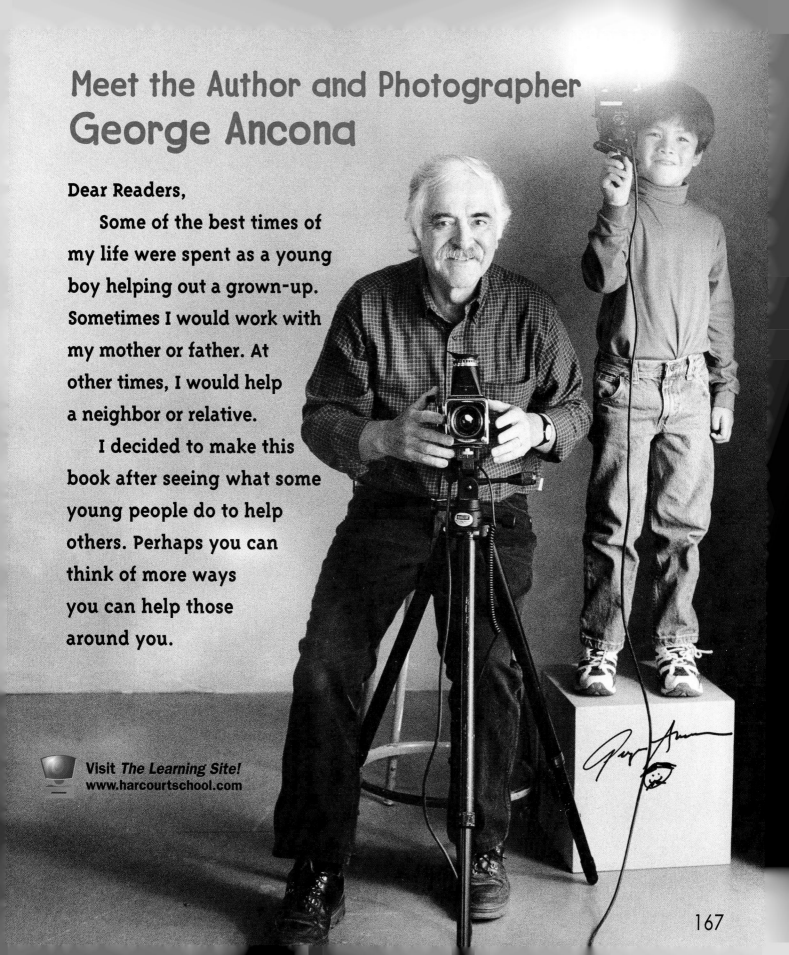

Meet the Author and Photographer
George Ancona

Dear Readers,

Some of the best times of my life were spent as a young boy helping out a grown-up. Sometimes I would work with my mother or father. At other times, I would help a neighbor or relative.

I decided to make this book after seeing what some young people do to help others. Perhaps you can think of more ways you can help those around you.

ALL JOIN IN

by Quentin Blake

When we're cleaning
up the house
We ALL JOIN IN

When we're trying
to catch a mouse
We ALL JOIN IN

When we've got some
tins of paint
We ALL JOIN IN

And when Granny's
going to faint
We ALL JOIN IN

And if Ferdinand decides to make
a chocolate fudge banana cake
What do we do? For goodness sake!

We ALL JOIN IN

Response Activities

Plan a Helping-Out Week Make a schedule

The children in this story do many things to help out. You can plan to help out, too.

Make a calendar that shows every day of the week. Under each day, write a sentence about how you can help your teacher, your family, or your friends. Cut out seven stars. If you helped out as you planned, give yourself a star for the day!

Thursday	Friday
I can help Mom dry the dishes.	I can help Mr. Stone pick up paper.

He Said, She Said

Write dialogue

Imagine that the people in this story are talking to each other. Work with a partner to write what they are saying.

1. Choose a photograph from the story.

2. Cut out speech balloons that look like this:

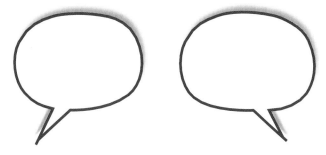

3. In the balloons, write what each person in the photograph is saying.

4. Do this for another photograph, too.

Share your speech balloons with classmates.

Mr. Putter and Tabby Fly

Award-Winning Author

the Plane

by Cynthia Rylant

illustrated by Arthur Howard

173

1

Toys

Mr. Putter loved toys.

He was old, and he knew

that he wasn't supposed

to love toys anymore.

But he did.

When Mr. Putter and his

fine cat, Tabby, drove into town,

they always stopped at the toy store.

Tabby was not happy at the toy store.
She was old, too,
and her nerves weren't as good
as they used to be.

The wind-ups made her twitch.
The pop-ups made her jump.

And anything that flew
gave her the hiccups.

But Tabby loved Mr. Putter,
so she put up with all of it.
While she twitched and jumped
and hiccuped, Mr. Putter
played with everything.
He played with the dump trucks.
He played with the cranes.
He played with the bear on the flying trapeze.

But most of all,

he played with the planes.

Ever since he was a boy
Mr. Putter had loved planes.
When he was young he had covered
his whole room with them.
Biplanes were his favorite,
but he also loved monoplanes
and seaplanes
and shiny ace Junkers.

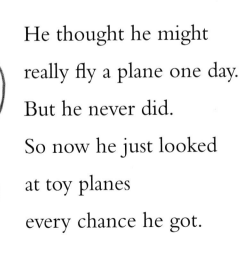

He thought he might
really fly a plane one day.
But he never did.
So now he just looked
at toy planes
every chance he got.

One day when
Mr. Putter and Tabby
were in the toy store and Tabby
was hissing at a wind-up penguin,
Mr. Putter spotted a plane
he had never seen before.

It was white and red, with
two wings on each side
and a little flag on its tail.
It was the most beautiful biplane
he had ever seen.
And it had a radio control
so a person might really fly it.

181

Mr. Putter was in love.

He bought the little plane and put it

in the car with Tabby.

He told her not to worry.

He promised her a nice cup of tea

with lots of cream

and a warm English muffin.

But still she hiccuped all the way home.

2

The Little Plane

Mr. Putter kept his promise.

He gave Tabby tea with cream and a warm

English muffin.

Then together they went outside

to fly his new plane.

Tabby had stopped hiccuping,
but only because she was full of tea.
She still didn't like Mr. Putter's plane.
Mr. Putter sat on the grass
and read all the directions.

Then he put the plane on the grass
and stepped back
and pressed the start button.
But the plane did not start.
It just rolled over and died.
Tabby purred.

Mr. Putter ran to the little plane.

He set it right again.

He told it to be a good little plane.

He stepped back

and pressed the start button.

But the plane did not start.

It fell on its nose and died.

Tabby purred and purred.

Mr. Putter ran to the plane.

He brushed the dirt off its nose.

He told it to be a brave little plane.

He stepped back

and pressed the start button.

But the plane did not start.

One of its wings fell off

and it died.

Tabby purred and purred and purred.

But poor Mr. Putter was so sad.

He picked up his little biplane.

He told the plane that it was

all his fault.

He told it that he was an old man

and old men shouldn't have toys anyway.

He said he wasn't any

good at flying planes.

Tabby watched Mr. Putter.

She could see that he was sad.

Then she felt sad, too.

Tabby went to Mr. Putter

and rubbed herself against his legs.

She sat on his shoulder,

put her head by his,

and licked his nose.

This made Mr. Putter feel better.

He decided to try again.

He fixed the wing.

He set the little plane on the grass.

He told it that he and Tabby knew
it was the best plane in the world.

Then he pressed the start button.

The little plane choked.

The little plane coughed.

The little plane gagged.

But it didn't die.

It warmed up and began to sound better.

Then slowly, slowly, it rolled across the grass.

It picked up speed. . . .

And then it *flew*!

It flew high into the blue sky.

Mr. Putter cheered. Tabby purred and hiccuped.

Mr. Putter was finally flying a plane of his own!

Think About It

1 How does Tabby help Mr. Putter fly his plane?

2 Think of your favorite toy. Why is it your favorite?

3 How can you tell that Mr. Putter and Tabby are good friends?

Cynthia Rylant

Dear Readers,

I love to write. I think that writing books adds beauty to the world. There are many other ways to add beauty, too, such as growing flowers, cooking delicious food, or raising sweet pets.

One of my pets is a cat named Blueberry. Blueberry likes only one thing—food!

♡ *Cynthia Rylant*

Arthur Howard

Dear Readers,

Before I illustrated this story, I thought a lot about Mr. Putter and Tabby. I asked myself what they would look like in a toy store or while flying a toy plane.

A lot of people ask me if I have a cat. I don't, but I love cats. I do have a pet hermit crab named Buster, though.

Visit *The Learning Site!*
www.harcourtschool.com

195

Response

Plane Facts

Research and report

Mr. Putter loved airplanes. Work with a group to give a report about airplanes.

1. Look for facts in books about airplanes or in an encyclopedia CD-ROM.

2. Write each fact on an index card.

3. Make a poster that shows your airplane facts.

4. Use your fact cards and poster to give a report about airplanes to classmates.

Some planes can carry more than 400 people.

Jet planes can fly faster than sound.

Biplanes have two pairs of wings.

Activities

Mr. Putter's New Toy

Draw a picture

What toy do you think Mr. Putter will buy next?
Draw a picture of it. Below your picture, write
some sentences that tell
about his new toy.
Add your picture to
a class toy catalog.

Hedgehog Bakes a Cake

by Maryann Macdonald  illustrated by Lynn Munsinger

Hedgehog was hungry for cake.
He found a yellow cake recipe.
"This one sounds easy," he said,
"and good, too."
Hedgehog took out the flour.

He took out the eggs and
the butter.

He was taking out the blue mixing bowl
when he heard a knock at the door.
It was Rabbit.
"Hello, Rabbit," said Hedgehog.
"I am making a cake."

"I will help you," said Rabbit.
"I am good at making cakes."
"Here is the recipe," said Hedgehog.
"You do not need this recipe," Rabbit said.
"I will show you what to do."

Rabbit took the flour.

He dumped it into the blue bowl.

He took the butter and dumped that in, too.

Then he dumped in the sugar.

"Now we will mix it," said Rabbit.

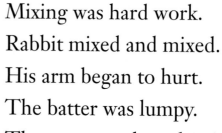

Mixing was hard work.
Rabbit mixed and mixed.
His arm began to hurt.
The batter was lumpy.
The sugar stuck to the sides of the bowl.
There was flour everywhere.
"I think someone is calling me,"
said Rabbit.
"You finish the mixing, Hedgehog.
I will come back
when the cake is ready."
Hedgehog shook his head.
The cake batter was a mess.

"What's the matter, Hedgehog?" Squirrel was at the door, looking in.

"I am making a cake," said Hedgehog.
"But it does not look very good."
"You need eggs," said Squirrel.
"I will put them in."
He cracked some eggs
and dropped them in.
Some shell fell in, too.

"A little bit of shell does not matter," said Squirrel. "Mix it all together." So Hedgehog mixed. The batter was more lumpy, but mixing was easier than before.

207

Owl stuck her head in the door.
"Baking?" she asked. "May I help?"
Hedgehog did not want more help.
But he didn't want to hurt Owl's feelings.

"You can butter the pan,"
said Hedgehog. Owl was happy.
She stuck her wing into the
butter. Then she smeared it
around the pan.

Owl turned on the oven
with her buttery feathers.
She turned it up as high
as it would go.
"The oven must be nice
and hot," she said.

"We have gotten very messy
helping you," said Squirrel.
"We will go home now and clean up.
Put the cake in the oven.
We will come back when it is ready."
Squirrel and Owl went home.

HEDGEHOG

Hedgehog looked at the kitchen.
There was sugar on the floor.
There was butter on the oven door.
And there was flour on everything.

Hedgehog dumped the cake batter
into the garbage pail.

He locked the kitchen
door and took out
his recipe.

First Hedgehog measured the sugar.
He mixed it slowly with the butter.
Next he counted out three eggs
and cracked them into the bowl—
one, two, three.
Then he added the flour.

211

Hedgehog mixed everything together and poured it into Owl's buttery pan.
He turned down the heat and put the batter in the oven.

Then he cleaned up the kitchen.

Knock, knock, knock.
"Open the door, Hedgehog," called Rabbit.
"We can smell the cake, and we are getting hungry."
Hedgehog unlocked the door. The kitchen was clean.
The cake was cooling on a rack. And the table was set for a tea party.

The four friends sat down.

Hedgehog cut the cake.

They each ate one slice.

Then they each ate another slice.

"This is the best cake I have ever made," said Rabbit.

"Aren't you glad I showed you how to do it?"

"The eggs made it very rich," said Squirrel.

"And you can't taste the shell at all."

"It's perfect," said Owl.

"I set the oven just right."

"Thank you all for your help," said Hedgehog.

"Next time I will try to do it all by myself."

Think About It

1 What happens when Hedgehog and his friends work together to bake a cake?

2 What do you like best about this story?

3 Why doesn't Hedgehog tell his friends he baked a new cake?

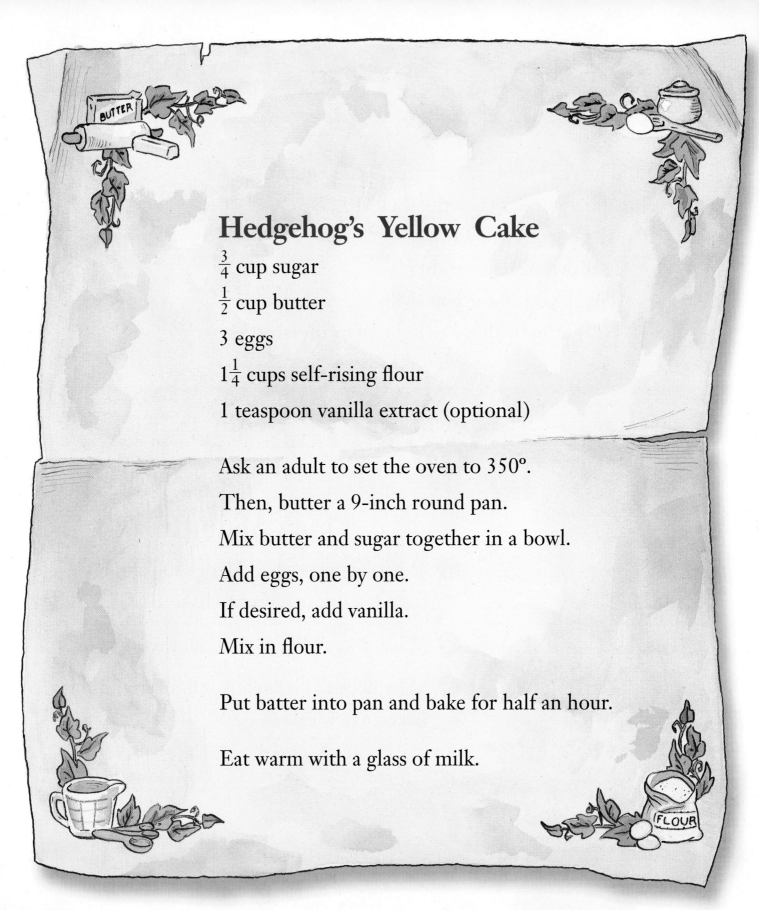

Hedgehog's Yellow Cake

$\frac{3}{4}$ cup sugar

$\frac{1}{2}$ cup butter

3 eggs

$1\frac{1}{4}$ cups self-rising flour

1 teaspoon vanilla extract (optional)

Ask an adult to set the oven to 350°.

Then, butter a 9-inch round pan.

Mix butter and sugar together in a bowl.

Add eggs, one by one.

If desired, add vanilla.

Mix in flour.

Put batter into pan and bake for half an hour.

Eat warm with a glass of milk.

Meet the Author and Illustrator
Maryann Macdonald

Maryann Macdonald has been around children most of her life. She grew up in a family of ten people. This helps her see things the way children do. As a young girl, Maryann Macdonald liked to listen to family stories. She soon began telling stories of her own. She published her first story when she was sixteen years old.

Lynn Munsinger

Lynn Munsinger illustrates magazines, school books, and greeting cards, but her favorite projects are children's books. She says, "I have wanted to be an artist for as long as I can remember. I really enjoy my work and cannot imagine doing anything else."

Visit *The Learning Site!*
www.harcourtschool.com

217

Response Activities

On Stage Perform a skit

Work with a group to act out "Hedgehog Bakes a Cake."

1. Decide who will play each character.

2. Make props to use in your play.

3. Practice your play.

Put on your play for others.

How-To Tips Make a list

What tips would Hedgehog give to someone who is baking for the first time? Make a list of tips on a sheet of paper. At the bottom, draw a picture about one of the tips.

Share your tips with classmates.

1. Always follow the recipe.

2. Clean up if you make a mess.

219

Synonyms and Antonyms

Reread this sentence from "Hedgehog Bakes a Cake."

Owl was happy.

Think of a word that means the opposite of *happy*. Words that have opposite meanings are called **antonyms**. The words in the first column of the chart are antonyms of *happy*:

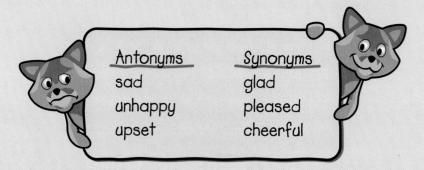

Antonyms	Synonyms
sad	glad
unhappy	pleased
upset	cheerful

Words that mean almost the same as another word are called **synonyms**. The words in the second column of the chart are synonyms of *happy*.

Writers use synonyms to make the meaning of a sentence clear. Look at the picture and read the sentence.

The fox walks through the woods.

WALKS

A writer can use a synonym for the word *walks*, such as *paces* or *wanders*. The synonyms help you understand what is happening.

The fox paces through the woods.
The fox wanders through the woods.

As you read, thinking about synonyms and antonyms can help you better understand the meaning of sentences.

WHAT HAVE YOU LEARNED?

Reread this sentence from the story:
"Open the door, Hedgehog," called Rabbit.

1 What is a synonym for the word *called*?

2 What is an antonym for the word *open*?

3 How would synonyms or antonyms change the meaning of the sentence?

TRY THIS • TRY THIS • TRY THIS

Look back at another story that you have read. Find a sentence with a word that has a synonym you know. Write the sentence with the synonym. Do the same for a sentence with a word that has an antonym you know. How did the meaning of the sentences change?

Visit *The Learning Site!*
www.harcourtschool.com

Lemonade

by Stuart J. Murphy

illustrated by Tricia Tusa

for Sale

Lemonade
for Sale

BY Stuart J. Murphy
ILLUSTRATED BY Tricia Tusa

Award-Winning
Illustrator

The members of the Elm Street Kids' Club were feeling glum.

"Our clubhouse is falling down, and our piggybank is empty," Meg said.

"I know how we can make some money," said Matthew. "Let's sell lemonade."

225

Danny said, "I bet if we can sell about 30 or 40 cups each day for a week, we'll make enough money to fix our clubhouse. Let's keep track of our sales."

Sheri said, "I can make a bar graph. I'll list the
number of cups up the side like this. I'll show the
days of the week along the bottom like this."

On Monday they set up their corner stand. When people walked by, Petey, Meg's pet parrot, squawked "Lemonade for sale! Lemonade for sale!"

Matthew squeezed the lemons.

Meg mixed in some sugar.

Danny shook it up with ice and poured it into cups.

Sheri kept track of how many cups they sold.

Sheri announced, "We sold 30 cups today. I'll fill in the bar above Monday up to the 30 on the side."

"Not bad," said Danny.

"Not bad. Not bad," chattered Petey.

229

On Tuesday Petey squawked again, "Lemonade for sale! Lemonade for sale!" and more people came by.

Matthew squeezed more lemons.

Meg mixed in more sugar.

Danny shook it up with ice and poured it into more cups.

Sheri kept track of how many cups they sold.

Sheri shouted, "We sold 40 cups today. I'll fill
in the bar above Tuesday up to the number 40.
The bars show that our sales are going up."

"Things are looking good," said Meg.

"Looking good. Looking good,"
chattered Petey.

On Wednesday Petey squawked "Lemonade for sale!" so many times that most of the neighborhood stopped by.

Matthew squeezed even more lemons.

Meg mixed in even more sugar.

Danny shook it up with ice and poured it into even more cups.

Sheri kept track
of how many cups they sold.

Sheri yelled, "We sold 56 cups today.
I'll fill in Wednesday's bar up to a little
more than halfway between 50 and 60."

"That's great," shouted Matthew.
"That's great! That's great!"
bragged Petey.

They opened again on Thursday, but something was wrong. No matter how many times Petey squawked "Lemonade for sale!" hardly anyone stopped by.

Matthew squeezed just a few lemons.

Meg mixed in only a couple of spoonfuls of sugar.

Danny's ice melted while he waited.

Sheri kept track of the few cups that they sold.

Sheri said, "We sold only 24 cups today. Thursday's bar is way down low."

"There goes our clubhouse," said Danny sadly. Petey didn't make a sound.

"I think I know what's going on," said Matthew.
"Look!" He pointed down the street.
"There's someone juggling on that corner,
and everyone's going over there to watch."

"Let's check it out," said Meg.

Danny asked the juggler, "Who are you?"
"I'm Jed," said the juggler. "I just moved here."

Sheri had an idea. She whispered
something to Jed.

On Friday, Sheri arrived with Jed.

"Jed's going to juggle right next to our stand,"
Sheri said.

That day Petey squawked, Jed juggled, and
more people came by than ever before.

Matthew squeezed
loads of lemons.

Meg mixed in tons
of sugar.

Danny shook it up
with lots of ice and
almost ran out of cups.

Sheri could hardly keep track
of how many cups they sold.

"We sold so many cups today
that our sales are over the top.
We have enough money to rebuild our clubhouse."

"Hooray!" they all shouted. "Jed! Jed!
Will you join our club?"
"You bet!" said Jed.
"You bet! You bet!" squawked Petey.

Think About It

1 How did the children work together to rebuild
their clubhouse?

2 If you were a member of a club, what could you
do to help raise money?

3 Why do you think the author used bar graphs in
the story?

Meet the Author and the Illustrator

Stuart J. Murphy

Stuart Murphy didn't enjoy math when he was young. But his feelings have changed. He now writes stories that show math ideas. He wants his stories to help children have fun as they learn math.

Stuart Murphy lives in Illinois with his wife. He loves to plan vacations—and to take them, too!

Tricia Tusa

Tricia Tusa has been a writer and illustrator of children's books since 1984. She is also an art therapist. She uses art to help children who are sad or hurt. She likes to show in her books that "it's okay to be different." Tricia Tusa lives in Houston, Texas.

Visit *The Learning Site!*
www.harcourtschool.com

241

Lemonade

Lemons all are yellow.

Lemons are afraid.

So squeeze a lemon gently

And give a lemonade.

by Pyke Johnson, Jr.

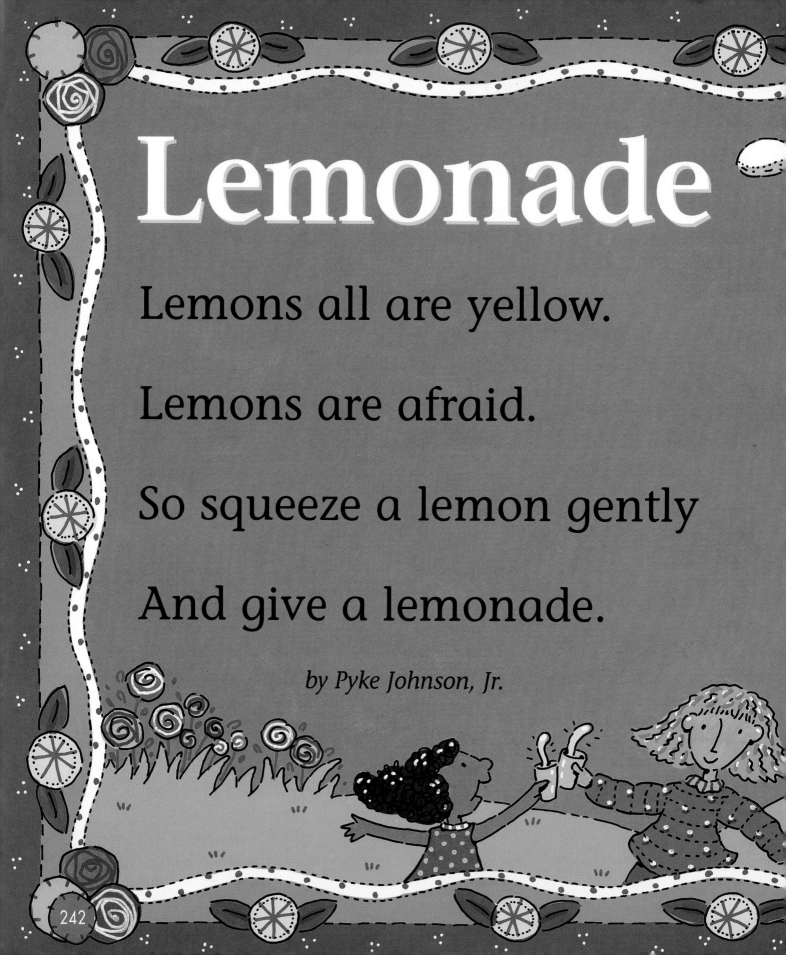

Response Activities

Thirsty? Make a graph

Work with a partner. Make a graph of your classmates' favorite drinks.

1. Think of three or four drinks, and list them.

2. Ask your classmates which of the drinks is their favorite.

3. Show their answers on a graph.

Share your results with classmates.

Come One, Come All!

Make a poster

The club members want to raise money by selling lemonade. Pretend you are a member of the club. Make a poster to tell about your lemonade stand. Make your poster fun and interesting. Write sentences on your poster telling people why they should buy your lemonade.

Share your poster with classmates.

Lend a Hand

CONNECT THEMES ACROSS TEXTS
The title of this theme is "Helping Hands." On a sheet of paper, trace an outline of one of your hands. On each finger, write the title of one of the stories in this theme. On the palm, write about how the characters worked together in the stories. Share your hand with your classmates.

Go for the Goal!

ANALYZE STORIES   The stories in this theme are all about working together to reach a goal. Choose one story from this theme and tell what goal the characters tried to reach. Give examples from the story. Share your ideas with classmates.

What a Character!

CHARACTER STUDY   Get together with a few classmates. Think about the characters in the stories. How would you describe each character or group of characters? Would you use words like *friendly*, *shy*, *talented*, and *smart*? Make a poster for each of these words. Write one word at the top of each poster. Below the word, draw pictures of characters the word describes.

CONTENTS

248

THEME

Our World

Reader's Choice

Flowers, Fruits, Seeds
by Jerome Wexler

NONFICTION

Photographs of plants and trees show the cycle from flower to fruit to seed to flower.

Award-Winning Author
READER'S CHOICE LIBRARY

Stellaluna
by Janell Cannon

FICTION

A baby bat falls into a bird's nest and is raised as a bird.

Award-Winning Author
READER'S CHOICE LIBRARY

Somewhere in the World Right Now
by Stacey Schuett

INFORMATIONAL FICTION

Right now, many things are happening around the world.

This Year's Garden
by Cynthia Rylant

REALISTIC FICTION

Follow the seasons of the year in a family's garden.

Award-Winning Author

Feel the Wind
by Arthur Dorros

NONFICTION

Learn about where the wind comes from and what it does in our world.

Outstanding Science Trade Book

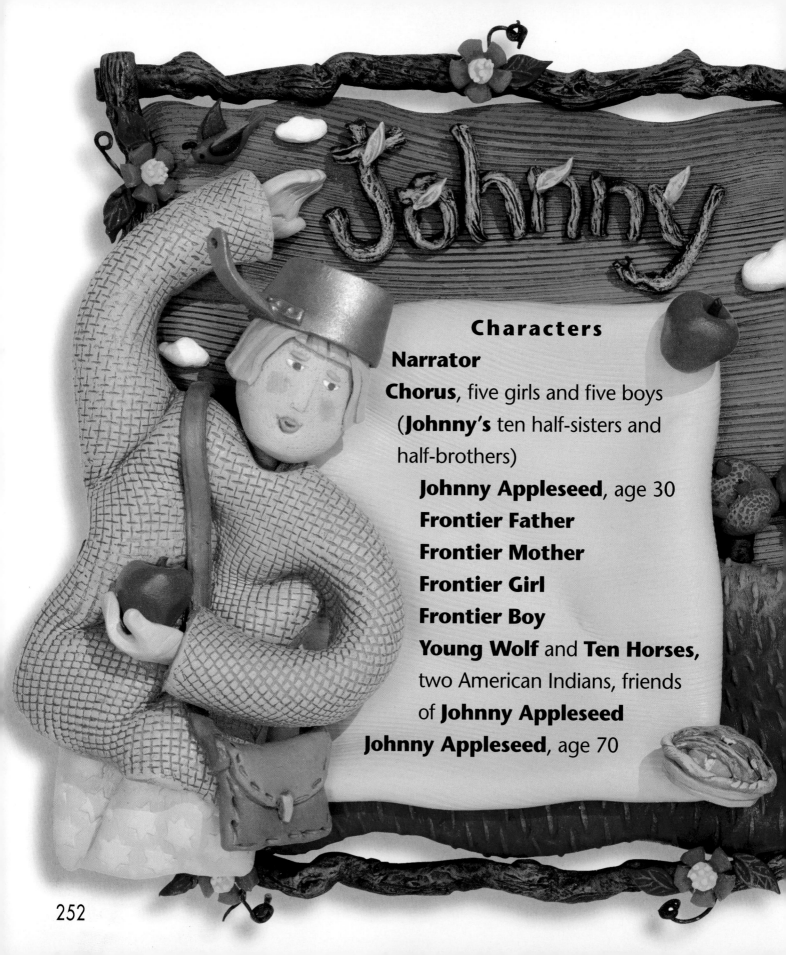

Johnny

Characters

Narrator

Chorus, five girls and five boys
(**Johnny's** ten half-sisters and
half-brothers)

    Johnny Appleseed, age 30

    Frontier Father

    Frontier Mother

    Frontier Girl

    Frontier Boy

    Young Wolf and **Ten Horses**,
two American Indians, friends
of **Johnny Appleseed**

Johnny Appleseed, age 70

Appleseed

an American Legend
adapted by Pleasant deSpain
illustrated by Victoria Raymond

Scene One

Time: Long ago.

Setting: Clearing in the woods. **Narrator** sits on a hollow log. **Johnny**, age 30, barefoot and wearing a stew pot on his head, munches on an apple. **Chorus** is nearby.

Narrator: This is the story of John Chapman, a true American hero. You might know him as Johnny Appleseed. Johnny was born in Massachusetts a long time ago. He had ten half-brothers and half-sisters.

Chorus: (*waves*) That's us!

Narrator: When Johnny was a boy, many of his neighbors were moving out west. They were pioneers on the wild frontier. Johnny decided that when he became a man, he would also go out west. He wanted to plant apple seeds everywhere he went. That way, the pioneers would have apples to eat at their new homes.

Narrator: Johnny left home at age 23.

Chorus: What did he take with him?

Narrator: He took a pot for cooking and a sack of apple seeds. He walked and walked and he planted and planted.

Chorus: He walked and walked and he planted and planted.

Narrator: 'Cause he had itchy feet!

Chorus: 'Cause he had itchy feet!

Narrator: Now Johnny is 30 years old. He hates to wear shoes, and he likes to sleep outdoors. He likes animals as much as he does people. He has been walking west and planting apple orchards for seven years now.

Chorus: Apple juice and apple butter. Apple sauce and apple cobbler. My, oh my, sweet apple pie! Yummmmmmmmmmmmm!

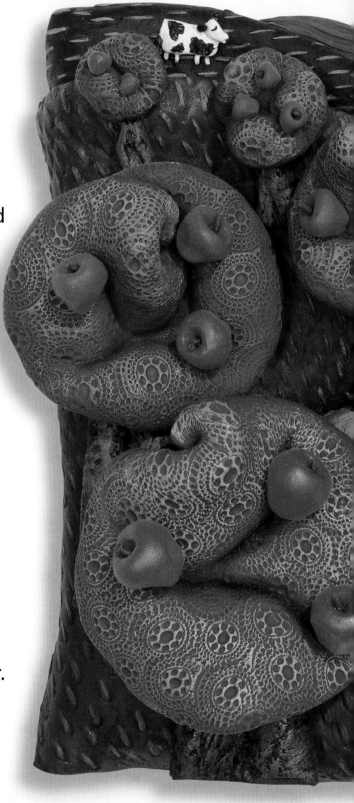

*(**Frontier Family** walks into the clearing.)*

Johnny: Howdy, folks! Come on over and rest a spell.

Frontier Girl: Pa, that man is wearing a pot on his head.

Frontier Boy: He looks strange, Ma!

Johnny: Don't be scared. People call me Johnny Appleseed.

Frontier Father: *(surprised)* We heard about you in Pennsylvania, and now here you are in Ohio.

Johnny: It's these itchy feet of mine. I have to keep moving west.

Frontier Mother: You planted all the apple trees we have seen along the way.

Frontier Father: That's hard work. Who pays you?

Johnny: *(laughs)* Nature does. I plant the orchards before folks move west so the apples are already growing when they arrive. The apples are nature's gift, and I just pass it along.

Frontier Girl: Pa says we are going to build a cabin and live here.

Frontier Boy: Where is your cabin, Johnny?

Johnny: (*laughs*) All around you. The earth is my floor, and the sky is my roof. The sun and wind and rain are my friends. This stew pot keeps my head dry, and wherever I go, I have all I need.

Frontier Mother: Don't you get cold?

Frontier Girl: Don't you get scared?

Frontier Boy: Don't you get lonely?

Johnny: Yes, yes, and yes. That's part of living outdoors, but I make friends wherever I go. My Indian friends have taught me how to survive in the great outdoors.

*(**Young Wolf** and **Ten Horses** walk into the clearing.)*

Johnny: Hello, Young Wolf and Ten Horses.

Young Wolf: Hello, Tree Planter. Who are these strangers?

Johnny: Meet my new friends. They came by wagon all the way from New England. They want to build a cabin here. They are good folks and good neighbors.

Frontier Father: Johnny's right. We promise to be good neighbors.

Young Wolf: Tree Planter always speaks the truth. Welcome, friends!

*(**Frontier Family** cheers.)*

Ten Horses: Be careful of the she-bear, Tree Planter.

*(**Young Wolf** and **Ten Horses** walk off.)*

Frontier Children: *(frightened)* The she-bear?

Johnny: Yes, I've heard her growl a time or two, but I get along with bears just fine.

Frontier Father: We must get back to the wagon. Thanks for everything, Johnny Appleseed.

*(**Frontier Family** walks off through the trees.)*

Johnny: *(yawns and stretches)* I'm so tired. I'll sleep in this hollow log tonight and finish planting the apple orchard tomorrow.

(**Johnny** *starts to crawl into the log.*)

Narrator: *(roars like a bear)* Grrrrrrrrrrr!

Johnny: *(startled)* I'm sorry Mrs. Bear!
I didn't know that this was your bed, too.
I'll sleep under the tree over there. You have
sweet dreams, you hear?

Narrator: *(growls warmly)* Mmmmm!

(**Johnny** *sits under tree and sleeps.*)

Scene Two

Time: *Many years later.*

Setting: *Narrator* and *Chorus* *are standing in an apple orchard.*

266

Narrator: Johnny Appleseed is now 70 years old. He's walked a long way, and he's still going.

Chorus: Apple juice and apple butter.
Apple sauce and apple cobbler.
My, oh my, sweet apple pie!
Yummmmmmmmmmmmmm!

(*Johnny, with a long white beard and a pot on his head, walks into the orchard. He carries a bag of seeds over his shoulder and a bright red apple in his hand.*)

Chorus Girls: How far did you walk, Johnny?

Johnny: Must be thousands of miles.

Chorus Boys: How long did it take?

Johnny: It took almost fifty years.

Chorus Boys: How many trees did you plant?

Johnny: Too many to count.

Chorus Girls: Who eats all the apples?

Johnny: The good folks who move out west looking for a better life.

Chorus: Do you still have itchy feet?

Johnny: *(laughs)* I was born with itchy feet. Got to keep on going, that's what I always say. This great new country needs lots of apples. They help us grow strong and healthy.

*(**Johnny** bites into apple and slowly begins to walk away.)*

Chorus: Good-bye, Johnny Appleseed.

Johnny: May you always be blessed with apples.

Chorus Girls: Thank you, Johnny Appleseed.

Chorus Boys: Be careful of the bears.

(*Johnny* *waves good-bye and walks out of sight.*)

Narrator: John Chapman died when he was 71 years old. We will never forget this pioneer and American hero.

Chorus Girls: Appleseed Johnny, Johnny Appleseed. John Chapman was his real name. The wild frontier he helped to tame.

Chorus Boys: He planted apple seeds, which grew into trees. This was his story. Everyone clap now, please.

(**Chorus** bows.)

The End

Think About It

1 How did Johnny Appleseed help the pioneers?

2 Would you like to live outdoors as Johnny Appleseed did? Why or why not?

3 Why do you think the author used a narrator in the play?

Meet the Author
Pleasant deSpain

Pleasant deSpain wrote his first story when he was eight years old. He's been writing and telling stories ever since. When Pleasant deSpain visits schools, he likes to act out stories in front of a class. That's why he wrote "Johnny Appleseed" as a play.

Meet the Illustrator
Victoria Raymond

Victoria Raymond uses clay to make her illustrations. She twists, pulls, rolls, and pounds the clay to give it the shape she wants. She uses the bark or leaves from trees to make impressions, or marks, in the clay. Like Johnny Appleseed, she and her family are moving out west.

Visit *The Learning Site!*
www.harcourtschool.com

271

Response

Puppet Show! Perform a puppet play

Plan a puppet show for the play "Johnny Appleseed."
Work with a group to make stick puppets. Use the
puppets to put on the play.

- Choose a character.

- Draw the character on construction paper
  and cut it out.

- Tape the character to a craft stick
  or ruler.

- Practice the play.

Your group can perform your
puppet play for another class.

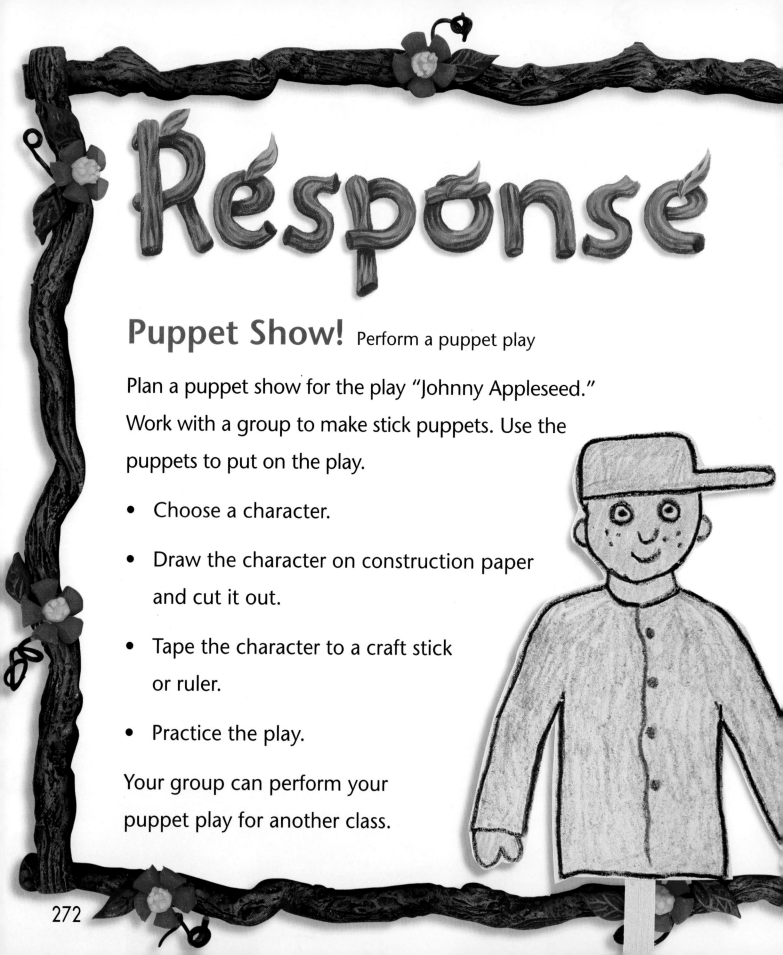

Activities

My Hero Write about a person

Johnny Appleseed was a true American hero because he helped the pioneers. Think about someone who is a hero to you. What is special about that person?

Draw a picture of that person. Write sentences that tell why that person is a hero.

My brother is my hero.
He teaches me new games.
He is a

From
Seed to Plant
by Gail Gibbons

Outstanding
Science
Trade Book

sunflower

oak tree

Most plants make seeds. A seed contains the beginning of a new plant. Seeds are different shapes, sizes and colors.

All seeds grow into the same kind of plant that made them.

apple tree

dandelion

zinnia

aster

Many plants grow flowers. Flowers are
where most seeds begin.

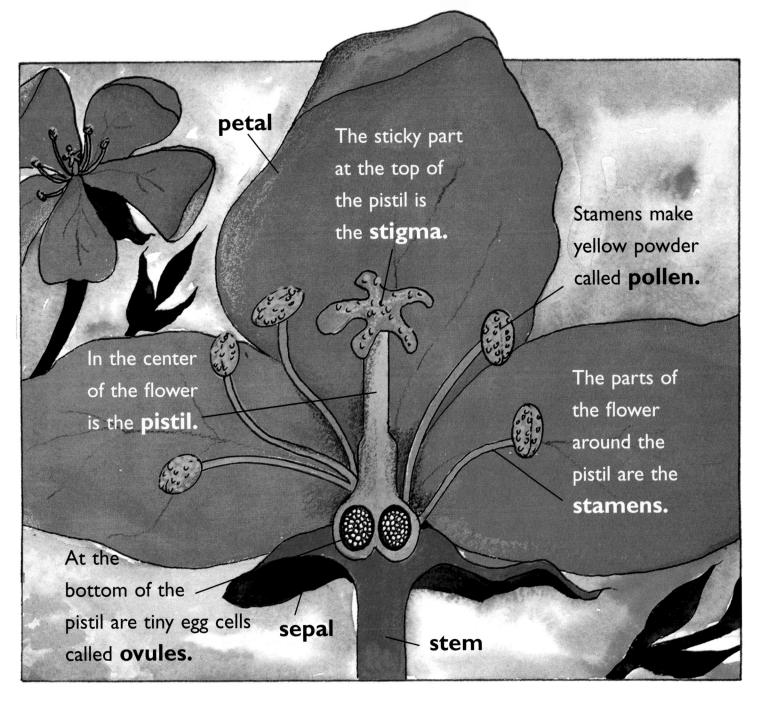

petal

The sticky part at the top of the pistil is the **stigma.**

Stamens make yellow powder called **pollen.**

In the center of the flower is the **pistil.**

The parts of the flower around the pistil are the **stamens.**

At the bottom of the pistil are tiny egg cells called **ovules.**

sepal

stem

A flower is made up of many parts.

Before a seed can begin to grow, a grain of pollen from the stamen must land on the stigma at the top of the pistil of a flower like itself. This is called pollination.

Pollination happens in different ways.
Often, wind blows pollen from flower to flower.

Bees, other insects and hummingbirds help pollinate, too. While they visit flowers for their sweet juice, called nectar, pollen rubs onto their bodies.

Then they carry the pollen to another flower where it comes off onto its pistil.

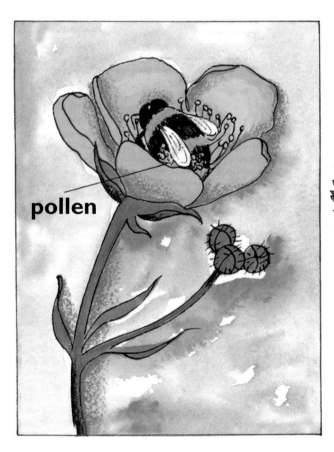

pollen

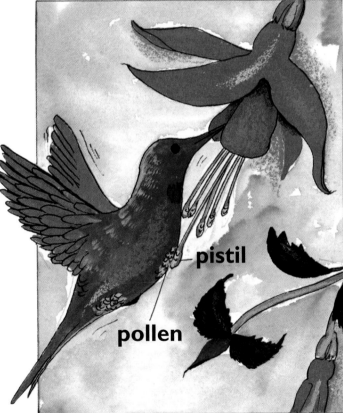

pistil

pollen

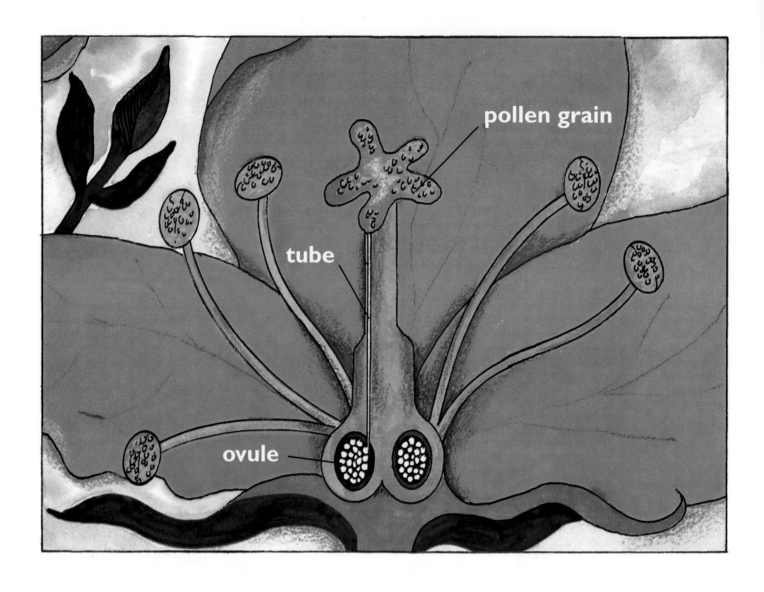

If a pollen grain from a flower lands on the pistil
of the same kind of flower, it grows a long tube
through the pistil into an ovule. This is the
beginning of a seed.

The seeds grow inside the flower, even as the flower begins to die. As the seeds become bigger, a fruit or pod grows around them. The fruit or pod protects the seeds.

When the fruit or pod ripens, it breaks open. The seeds are ready to become new plants.

Some seeds fall to the ground around the base of the plant where they will grow.

Some pods or fruits open and the seeds pop out.
Sometimes, when birds eat berries, they drop
the seeds.

Other seeds fall into streams, ponds, rivers or the
ocean. There, they travel on the water until they
stick to dirt along a shore.

The wind scatters seeds. Some seeds have
fluff on them that lets them float to the ground
like tiny parachutes. Others have wings that
spin as they fall.

Animals help scatter seeds, too. They hide acorns
and nuts in the ground. Some seeds have hooks
that stick to the fur of animals or people's
clothes. Later, they drop off onto the ground.

A flower bed or vegetable garden is beautiful!
Seeds are planted to grow in the gardens.

The seeds come in small envelopes or boxes.
Directions explain how to plant the seeds
and care for the plants.

The beginning of a plant is curled up inside
each seed. Food is stored inside the seed,
too. The seed has a seed coat on the outside
to protect it.

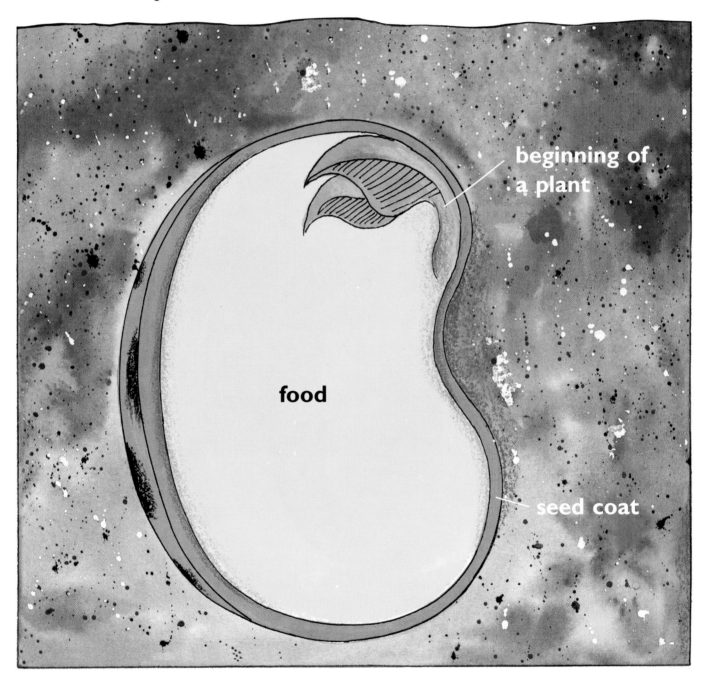

beginning of
a plant

food

seed coat

A seed will not sprout until certain things happen. First it must be on or in the soil. Then it needs rain to soak the seed and soften its seed coat.

When the sun shines and warms the ground,
the seed coat breaks open and the seed begins
to grow. This is called germination. A root grows
down into the soil. The root takes in water and
minerals from the soil for food.

Up grows a shoot. Green leaves grow up from
the shoot toward the sun.

The plant grows bigger and bigger. The leaves
make food for the plant from the water and
minerals in the soil, the sunlight, and the air
all around the plant.

Finally, the plant is full-grown. Buds on the plant open into flowers where new seeds will grow.

Many of the foods people eat are seeds, fruits and pods. They are full of nutrition, vitamins and minerals and they are tasty, too!

Think About It

1 How does a seed become a plant?

2 What did you learn from this story that you did not know before?

3 How are the illustrations in this nonfiction story different from the illustrations in a fiction story that you've read?

Meet the Author and Illustrator Gail Gibbons

What does Gail Gibbons need to make her books?

First, she needs ideas. She loves to write and illustrate nonfiction books. She says, "I learn a lot about the world I live in."

Next, Gail Gibbons needs time. It takes her about two months to draw all of the illustrations for one book.

What else does Gail Gibbons need? Lots of paper and plenty of paints!

Visit *The Learning Site!*
www.harcourtschool.com

A "From Seed

1. Find a clean glass jar. Take a piece of black construction paper and roll it up.

2. Slide the paper into the jar. Fill the jar with water.

3. Wedge the bean seeds between the black paper and the glass. Put the jar in a warm place.

BEANS

WATCHING YOUR BEAN SEEDS WHILE THEY SPROUT

4. In a few days the seeds will begin to sprout. Watch the roots grow down. The shoots will grow up.

to Plant" Project

CARING FOR
YOUR BEAN
PLANTS

5. Put dirt into a big clay pot.

6. Carefully remove the small plants from the glass jar. Place them in the soil, covering them up to the base of their shoots.

7. Water them . . . and watch them grow!

THINK ABOUT IT

Why is it useful for people to know how plants grow?

Response Activities

What Am I? Write a riddle

Write a plant riddle. Begin your riddle with "I began as a seed." Then tell where you were planted. What do you look like now? Tell about your size, color, and shapes. Do not tell what kind of plant you are. End your riddle with "What am I?" On the back of your riddle, write the answer.

Read your riddle to some classmates. Have them guess what you are.

Label It! Create a diagram

In the story, the parts of the plants are labeled. Labels help us understand pictures better. You can make a picture with labels.

1. Choose an object that has different parts. You might choose a tool, a toy, or an animal. Use an encyclopedia or books to get ideas.

2. Draw a picture of the object.

3. Label the parts of the object.

Share your picture with a group. Tell the group about the different parts of your object.

Award-Winning
Author

WATERM

by Kathi Appelt

illustrated by Dale Gottlieb

That watermelon grew in the corner of the patch where the fence posts met. Jesse found it early one day while pulling weeds. It was not as big as her fist, but it was bigger than the other melons still hiding beneath their mamas' fuzzy leaves.

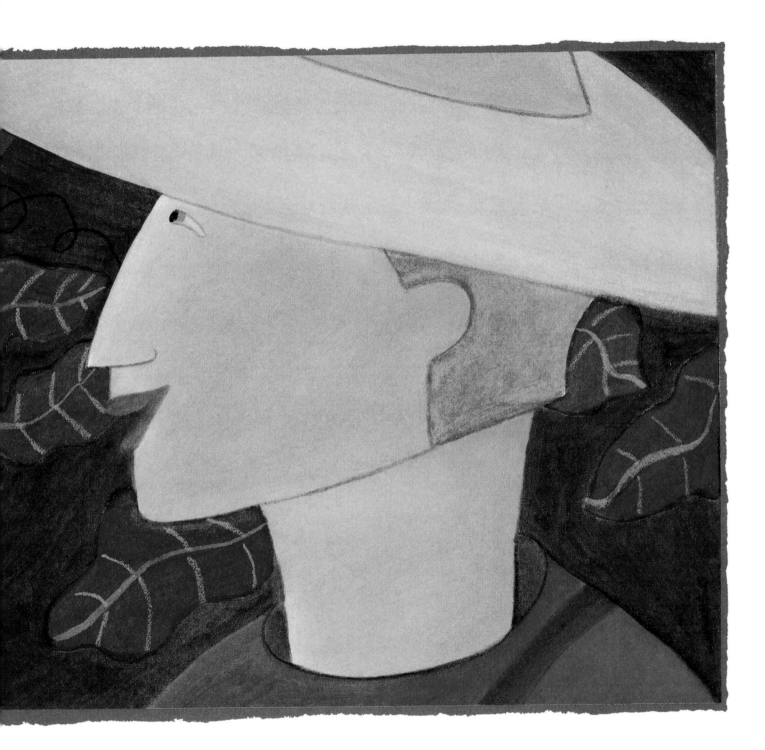

When she showed it to Pappy, he smiled. "Yep, it'll be a big one all right. It'll be just right for a Watermelon Day."

"A Watermelon Day!"

Jesse knew what that meant. There would be cousins, big and small. Mama's peach ice cream. Innings and innings of softball. Relay races and apple-bobbing. Uncle Ike with his banjo. Finally, to top it all, ice-cold watermelon—the biggest one from the patch.

Thinking about it made Jesse's mouth water.

"How long till it's ready, Pappy?" she asked.

"Got a whole summer to go yet," he answered.

Jesse looked at the small melon. It was round and snug in the sand. She smiled.

Every day Jesse walked up and down the rows of the
patch. When she got to her melon, she knelt beside it
and put her ear against its dark green rind.

She patted it with her palm. At first it made a thick, dull sound, like Pappy's boots when he dropped them on the front porch. But as the days passed, the sound grew brighter. Jesse patted the other melons, too. Some sounded dull. Some sounded bright. But hers had the sweetest song.

Watermelon, watermelon.

"How much longer, Pappy?" she asked.
"Not much longer now," he answered.

The summer days grew longer. Jesse's watermelon got riper. Its stripes began to zig and zag.

Jesse waited. She waited until the days were so hot she had to wear shoes so her feet wouldn't blister in the sand. So hot the air wrinkled up like an unironed shirt. So hot that hardly anything moved except the flies.

She waited until she thought she and her watermelon might both burst from the sheer waiting of it all.

One morning, when the relatives were coming, Jesse
asked, "How much longer, Pappy?" Pappy looked at Jesse.
He looked at the watermelon patch. He looked at the blue
summer sky. "Well," he answered, "this looks like a
Watermelon Day."

"A Watermelon Day!"

Jesse skipped to the corner of the patch where the fence
posts met. She patted her watermelon. It was full of the
cool summer rains. Full of the warmth from its sandy nest.
Full of the deep hot sun.

Pappy cut the ropelike vine with his pocketknife and carried the melon out of the patch, past the front porch and down to the lake. He set it in the cold, cold water. There it floated, right along the edge, beneath the deep blue shade of the weeping willow tree.

"How long will it take, Pappy?" asked Jesse.

"Most of the day," he answered. "There's a whole summer's worth of heat inside it."

Jesse's watermelon floated all that hot day long.
Willow branches dipped up and down, testing the icy
water. That melon floated while the cousins came.

It floated while Mama dished out peach ice cream.

It floated through a game of softball and several relay races.

It even floated while Uncle Ike played "Turkey in the Straw."

And all the while Jesse thought about it, her mouth watered.

Watermelon, watermelon.

"How much longer, Pappy?" she asked.
"Oh, it's not ready yet," he answered.

310

The day stretched and stretched like a lazy ol' cat. Jesse waited and waited.

She waited through more innings of softball. She waited through apple-bobbing. She waited through freeze-tag. She waited through Uncle Ike's rendition of "Stars and Stripes Forever."

At last the sun began to sink. The sweat dried on Jesse's neck. The lake shimmered. "How much longer, Pappy?" she asked. Pappy looked at Jesse. He looked at the sinking sun. He looked at the shimmery lake. "I think it's good and cold now," he answered.

Jesse hopped. She skipped. She danced all the way to the lake. Pappy lifted the melon out of the icy water and carried it to the front porch, where he set it down.

With the side of his fist, Pappy hit that melon right in the deep, deep middle.

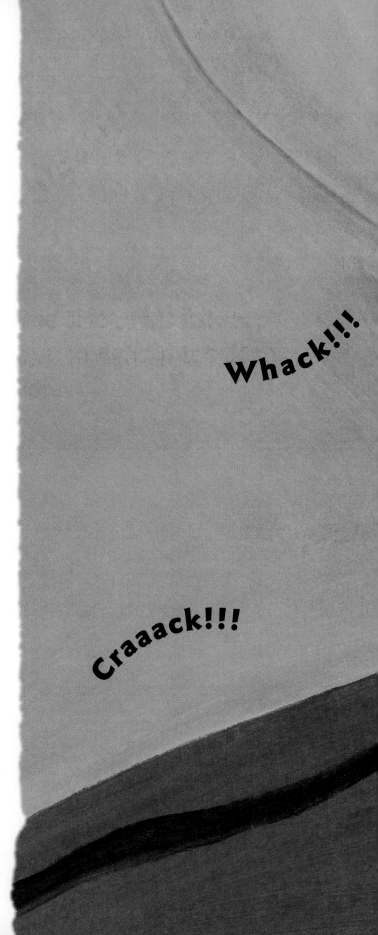

Whack!!!

Craaack!!!

313

Red, red juice ran down Jesse's chin. It ran down
her hand and between her fingers. It splashed onto
her toes.

That melon was sweet. Sweet as the summer rain. Sweet as a nighttime song. That melon was cold. Cold as a puppy's nose. Cold as the deep blue lake.

Jesse smiled. She danced. She spit watermelon seeds into the sky. She sang a watermelon song.

Watermelon, watermelon.

Think About It

1. How does Jesse feel about her watermelon?

2. If you could grow anything in a garden, what would it be? Why?

3. How does Jesse's watermelon help her understand the world of nature?

Meet the Author and the Illustrator

Kathi Appelt

Would your mother be upset if you drew on the walls? Kathi Appelt's mother wasn't. Kathi and her sisters drew pictures on the walls of their garage. Later, Kathi wrote poetry on the walls, too. She now lives in Texas with her family and writes children's books. But Kathi Appelt doesn't write on walls anymore. Now she uses a computer.

Dale Gottlieb

Besides illustrating children's books, Dale Gottlieb makes what she calls "story rugs." The pictures in the rugs tell stories. She gets ideas for her rugs from stories she reads and even the children's stories she writes. You can see her rugs in Seattle, Washington.

Visit *The Learning Site!*
www.harcourtschool.com

317

RESPONSE

SWEET AS HONEY Use similes

Jesse uses the word *as* to tell about her watermelon.
She says that the watermelon is "sweet as the summer rain,"
"cold as a puppy's nose," and "cold as the deep blue lake."

Pick one of your favorite fruits. Draw a picture of the fruit
at the top of a sheet of paper. Below your picture, write
three sentences about your fruit using the word *as*.

Share your picture and sentences
with classmates.

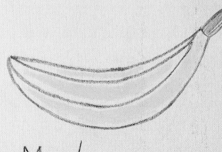

My banana is
as yellow as
the sun.

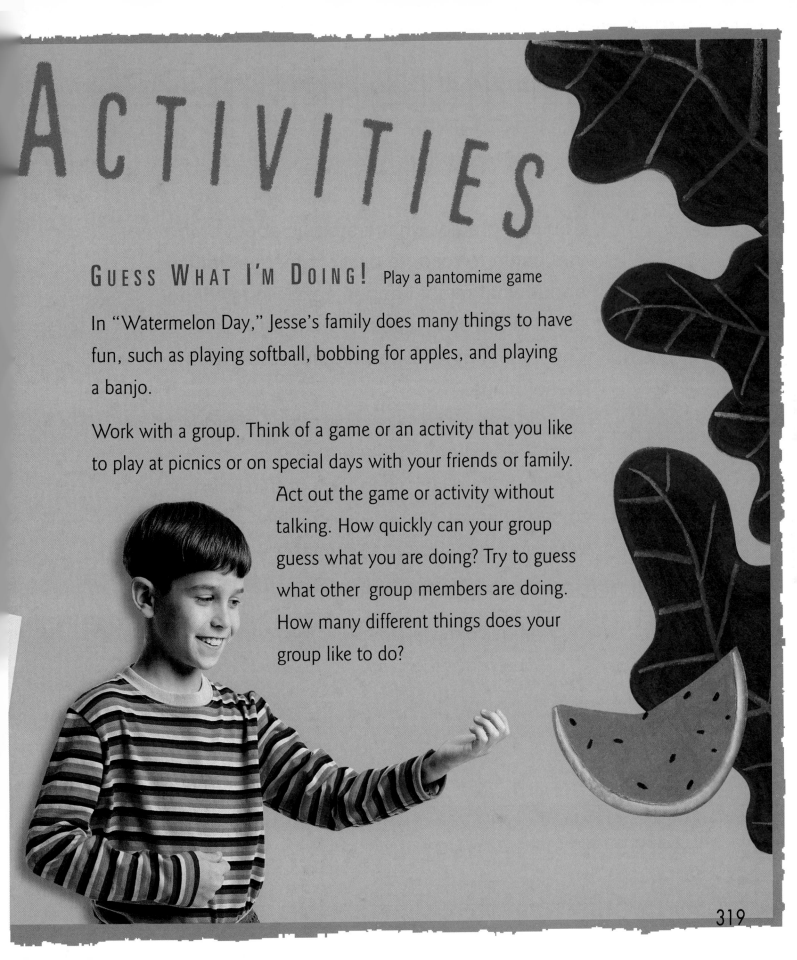

ACTIVITIES

GUESS WHAT I'M DOING! Play a pantomime game

In "Watermelon Day," Jesse's family does many things to have fun, such as playing softball, bobbing for apples, and playing a banjo.

Work with a group. Think of a game or an activity that you like to play at picnics or on special days with your friends or family. Act out the game or activity without talking. How quickly can your group guess what you are doing? Try to guess what other group members are doing. How many different things does your group like to do?

Predict Outcomes

You can predict what a story is about before you begin to read. To **predict** means to think about what might happen next. First, look for clues in the story title and in the illustrations. Then, think of what you already know about these things.

You can also make predictions as you read. Reread pages 298 and 299 of "Watermelon Day." Then look at this chart to see how you can use story clues and what you know to predict what will happen.

What will happen on Watermelon Day?

Story clues +	What I already know =	Prediction
Pappy says Jesse's watermelon will grow big. He says it will be just right for a Watermelon Day. Jesse and Pappy are smiling.	Ripe watermelons are juicy and sweet. They are fun to eat. People have parties on special days.	Jesse's watermelon will grow big and sweet. Watermelon Day will be a time for a special party. Watermelon Day will be a lot of fun.

As you read a story, think about the story events and the characters. Think about what you already know. Use these clues to help you predict what will happen next. You may want to change your predictions as you get new clues. The more information you get, the easier it is to make a good prediction.

WHAT HAVE YOU LEARNED?

1. Look back at pages 296 and 297 of "Watermelon Day." What clues did you find that helped you predict what this story is about?

2. Reread pages 312 and 313 of "Watermelon Day." What will the watermelon probably taste like? How do you know?

Visit *The Learning Site!*
www.harcourtschool.com

TRY THIS • TRY THIS • TRY THIS

Choose a book from your classroom or school library that you haven't read before. With a partner, read half of the book and stop.

Think about the story title and illustrations. Predict what will happen next in the story. Then finish reading the book. Talk with your partner about the story clues that helped you make your prediction.

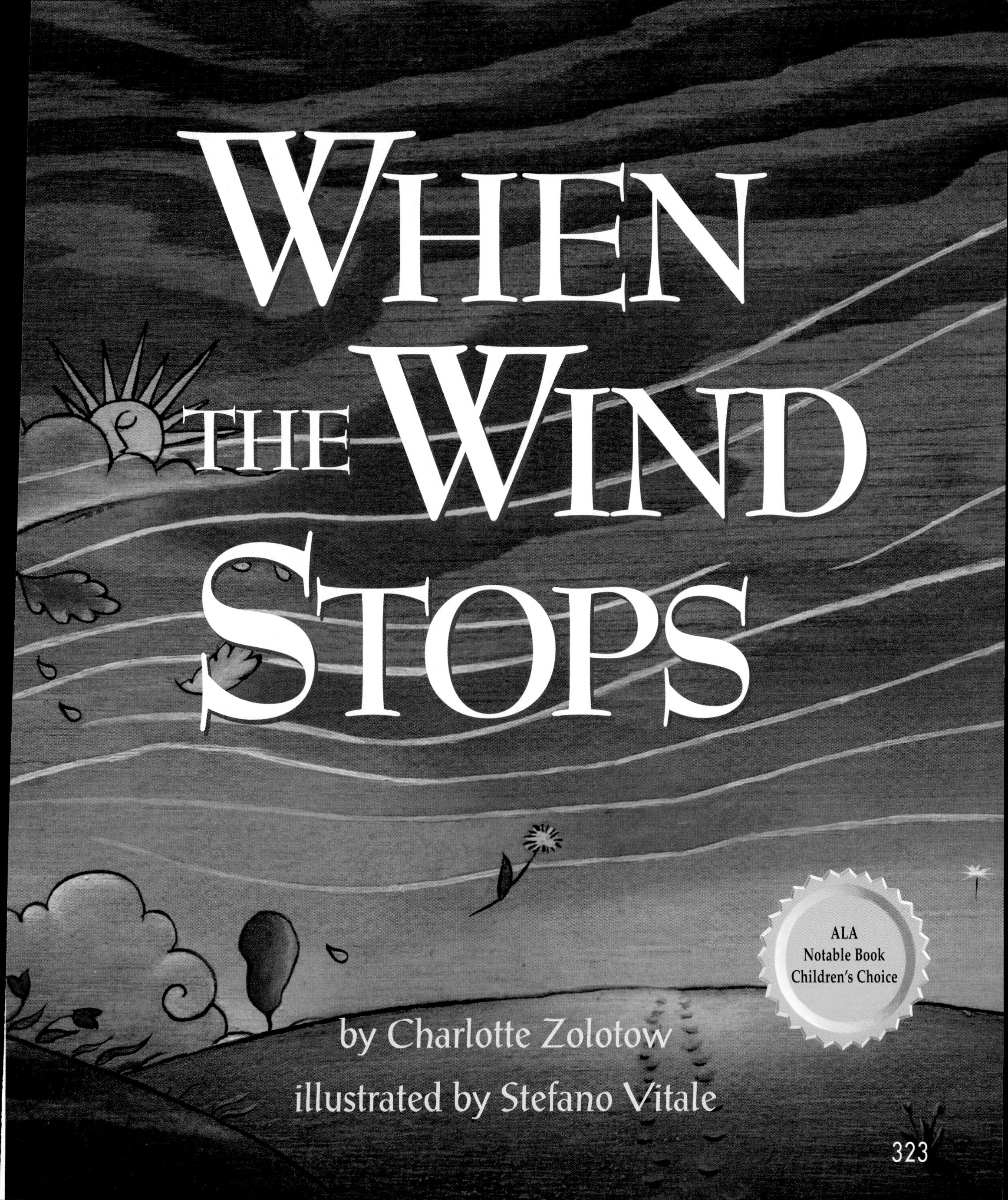

WHEN THE WIND STOPS

by Charlotte Zolotow

illustrated by Stefano Vitale

ALA
Notable Book
Children's Choice

The great bright yellow sun had shone all day, and now the day was coming to an end. The light in the sky changed from blue to pink to a strange dusky purple. The sun sank lower into the long glowing clouds.

The little boy was sorry to see the day end.

He and his friend had played in the garden.

When they were tired of playing, they lay down
in the grass and felt the sun on them, warm and soft,
like a sleepy cat resting.

There had been icy lemonade, in the afternoon,
which they drank under the pear tree.

And the little boy's father read him a story on the
porch before he went to bed.

Now his mother came to say good night.
"Why does the day have to end?" he asked her.
"So night can begin," she said, "look."
She pointed out the window where, high in the
darkening sky, behind the branches of the pear tree,
the little boy could see a pale sliver of moon.
"That's the night beginning," his mother
said, resting her hand on his shoulder,
"the night with the moon and stars
and darkness for you to dream in."

"But where does the sun go when the day ends?" the little boy asked.

"The day doesn't end," said his mother, "it begins somewhere else. The sun will be shining there, when night begins here. Nothing ends."

"Nothing?" the little boy asked.

"Nothing," his mother said. "It begins in another place or in a different way."

The little boy lay in bed, and his mother sat beside him.

"Where does the wind go when it stops?" he asked.

"It blows away to make the trees dance somewhere else."

"Where does the dandelion fluff go when it blows away?"

"It carries the seed of new dandelions to someone's lawn."

"Where does the mountain go after the top?"
"Down to where it becomes the valley."

"Where do waves go when they break on
the sand?"
"Sucked back to the sea into new waves."

"Where does the rain go when the storm is over?"

"Into clouds to make other storms."

"And where do clouds go when they move across the sky?"

"To make shade somewhere else."

"And the leaves in the forest when they turn color and fall?"

"Into the ground to become part of new trees with new leaves."

"But when the leaves fall, that is the end of something!" the little boy said. "It is the end of autumn."

"Yes," his mother said. "The end of autumn is when the winter begins."

"And the end of winter . . . ?" the little boy asked.

"The end of winter, when the snow melts and the birds come back, is the beginning of spring," his mother said.

The little boy smiled.

"It really does go on and on," he said.
"Nothing ends."

He looked out at the sky. The sun was gone completely. The lovely pink clouds had disappeared. The sky was dark and purple-black. High above the branches of the pear tree shone, clearly now, a thin new moon.

"Today is over," his mother said. "It's time for sleep, and tomorrow morning, when you wake, the moon will be beginning a night far away, and the sun will be here to begin a new day."

THINK ABOUT IT

1. What does the boy's mother tell him about nature?

2. If you were the boy, what else would you ask?

3. How do you think the boy feels at the end of the story?

339

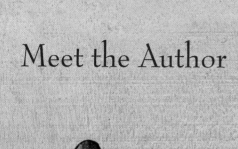

Charlotte Zolotow

Q. Do you have any special stories about your childhood?

A. I was born on my sister's sixth birthday. She was happy about this until she saw me. Then she cried and said she wished she had gotten a bicycle instead!

Q. When your children were young, did they give you any ideas for your books?

A. I got ideas from bedtime stories I told my son, Stephen, and from things we did together. My daughter, Ellen, makes me remember my own childhood.

Charlotte Zolotow

Meet the Illustrator
Stefano Vitale

Q. Did you ask questions like the boy in the story when you were a child?

A. Yes, but I always tried to find the answers by myself without asking my mother.

Q. What did you like most about painting the pictures for this book?

A. I liked using my imagination to picture the story in my mind.

Visit *The Learning Site!*
www.harcourtschool.com

341

Wind

Suddenly
A wind
Has come up,
Sending
The gray clouds
Flying.
And
Suddenly
It is
Such a beautiful day,
You can hear
The trees
Cheering.

by James Stevenson
Illustrated by Doug Bowles

RESPONSE ACTIVITIES

A WIND-SWEPT TALE Write a story

Write a story about an object that gets picked up by the wind and carried far, far away. Tell where it goes, what happens to it, and where it finally lands. Give your story a title. Share your wind-swept tale with classmates.

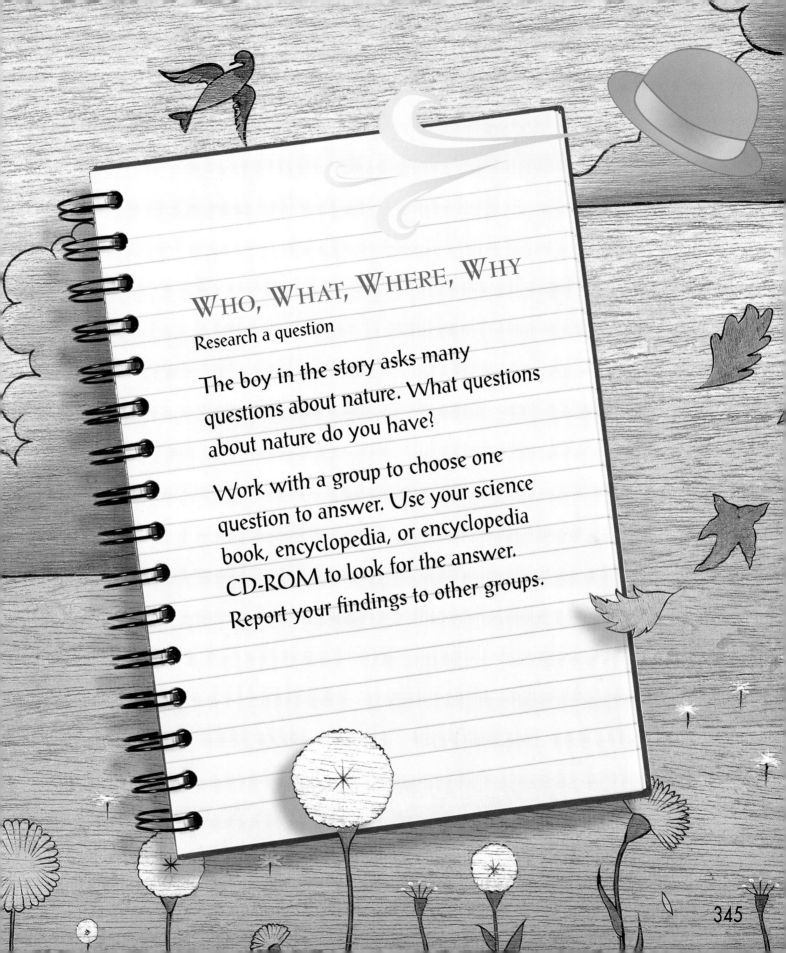

Who, What, Where, Why

Research a question

The boy in the story asks many questions about nature. What questions about nature do you have?

Work with a group to choose one question to answer. Use your science book, encyclopedia, or encyclopedia CD-ROM to look for the answer. Report your findings to other groups.

WHAT MAKES
DAY

Award-Winning
Author

by Franklyn M. Branley

illustrated by D. R. Greenlaw

AND NIGHT

We all live on the earth.

The earth is our planet.

It is round like a big ball.
And it is spinning.

It's hard to believe the
earth is always turning,
because we don't feel
any motion. This is because
the earth spins smoothly—
always at the same speed.

If you were way out in space and watching the earth, you would see it spin. The earth spins around once in twenty-four hours.

Light from the sun falls on one-half of the spinning earth. The half in the light has day. The other half is dark. It is in the earth's shadow. That half has night.

This is a photograph of the earth. It was taken by a camera aboard the Apollo 17 spacecraft. You can see that the earth is round.

As the earth spins we move through the light, into the darkness, and back again. We have day and night.

Imagine you are in a spaceship high above the North Pole. Imagine you can stay there twenty-four hours and watch the earth make one complete turn.

As the earth turns we have sunrise, daylight, sunset, and night.

You can see how we move from daylight to darkness by doing an experiment. You will be the earth, and a lamp will be the sun.

sunrise

day

Stand so that your left side is toward the lamp. Hold your arms out all the way. Your left hand points toward the lamp. This is sunrise.

Stay in the same spot. Keep your arms out from your sides, and turn to your left. Now the lamp is in front of you. It is the middle of the day. It is noontime.

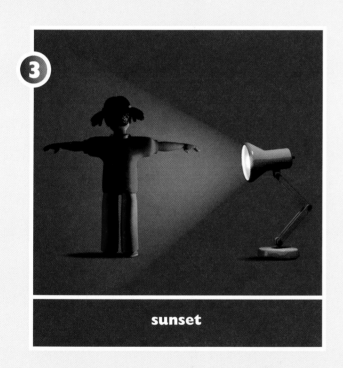

sunset

night

Keep turning until your right hand points toward the lamp. You are turning away from the light. It is sunset.

Keep turning until your back is toward the lamp. It is night. But your back is in daylight. Half of you is always light, and half is dark. It's the same with the earth.

The earth is always turning. It never stops. Round and round it goes. And it goes very fast. About 1000 miles an hour. As the earth turns we are always moving from day to night. And from night to day.

You can see this happen. If you are awake very early, you can see sunrise. The earth is moving you toward the sun.

The earth keeps turning. Later in the day we begin to turn away from the sun. You can see sunset.

About twenty-four hours after sunrise, the sun will rise again. It all happens because the earth is spinning around.

As the earth turns, the sun seems to move across the sky.

If you were on the moon, you would also have day and night. But the moon spins very slowly, so days and nights are long. Places on the moon have two weeks of daylight and then two weeks of darkness.

During one night on the moon the earth spins
around fourteen times.

14
LAPS

The turning earth gives us about twelve hours of daylight and twelve hours of darkness. That seems just about right for all of us on the planet earth.

Think About It

1 Why do we have day and night?

2 What is your favorite thing about day? What is your favorite thing about night?

3 Why do you think Franklyn Branley wrote this selection?

Meet the Author

Franklyn M. Branley

What Makes Day and Night is just
one of more than 130 children's science
books Franklyn Branley has written.
He knows a lot about day and night
because he has also been an astronomer.
Franklyn Branley still likes to gaze at
the stars from his home by the ocean.

Meet the Illustrator

D. R. Greenlaw

D. R. Greenlaw began making
comic books and animated
cartoons as a young boy.
After high school, he worked
as an illustrator for the
space program. D. R. Greenlaw
now works as an artist and
animator for feature motion
pictures.

 Visit *The Learning Site!*
www.harcourtschool.com

357

RESPONSE

Day and Night, Black and White Make a list

Think about things you see only in the daytime and things you see only at night. Make a list of these things.

1. Tape a sheet of black construction paper to a sheet of white construction paper.

2. With a white crayon, write a list of night things on the black paper.

3. With a black crayon, write a list of day things on the white paper.

Look in your science textbook for more things to add to your lists.

ACTIVITIES

Try It Yourself! Do an experiment

Work with a partner to do an experiment about night and day.

1. Get a flashlight and globe.

2. Put a self-stick note on the globe to show where you live.

3. Go to a dark corner of your classroom.

4. One partner shines the flashlight at the globe. The other partner slowly turns the globe.

When is it dark where you live? When is it light? Draw pictures and write about what you learned.

Stories like "What Makes Day and Night" have many details. **Details** are pieces of information that answer *who, what, where, when, how,* and *why* questions.

This web shows some details from "What Makes Day and Night."

It always spins.

It spins smoothly.

The earth spins.

It spins through the light, into the darkness, and back again.

Read the sentence in the center of the web. *The earth spins* is an important detail. You need to know this fact to understand what is happening in "What Makes Day and Night."

Now read the other three sentences in the web. These details give you more information about how the earth spins. They tell:

WHEN the earth spins (always)

HOW the earth spins (smoothly)

WHY we have day and night (the earth spins through the light and darkness)

These details make the story more interesting to read.

Some story details give you important facts. Other details make those facts more interesting. As you read a story, look for details that help you understand and enjoy it.

WHAT HAVE YOU LEARNED?

Reread pages 352 and 353 of "What Makes Day and Night."

1 What is the most important detail on these pages?

2 Which details make these pages more interesting?

Visit *The Learning Site!*
www.harcourtschool.com

TRY THIS • TRY THIS • TRY THIS

Look back at another story that you have read. Find details that are important and interesting. Write the details in a web. Talk to a partner about which details are most important and which ones make the story more interesting.

Theme Wrap-Up

Nature Facts

MAKE A TRADING CARD
Choose a fact about nature
that you learned from one
of the stories in this theme.
Draw a picture about this
fact on an index card.
Write a sentence about
the fact below the picture.
Trade your fact card with
a classmate. Tell why you
chose the fact you drew
and wrote about.

Get the Message?

UNDERSTAND AUTHOR'S MESSAGE Authors often want you to learn something from their stories. The authors in this theme want you to think about the world we live in. Choose a story from this theme. Write a note to your classmates telling what you think the author wanted to say through the story. Share your note.

I Didn't Know That!

DISCUSS THE LITERATURE Get together with a few classmates to discuss the stories in this theme. Talk about how the stories, project, and poem are alike and how they are different.

Using the Glossary

Get to Know It!

The **Glossary** gives the meaning of a word as it is used in the story. It also gives an example sentence that shows how to use the word. A **synonym**, which is a word that has the same meaning, a **base word**, or **additional word forms** may come after the example sentence. The words in the **Glossary** are in ABC order, also called **alphabetical order**.

Learn to Use It!

If you want to find *cranes* in the **Glossary**, you should first find the *C* words. *C* is near the beginning of the alphabet, so the *C* words are near the beginning of the **Glossary**. Then you can use the guide words at the top of the page to help you find the entry word *cranes*. It is on page 366.

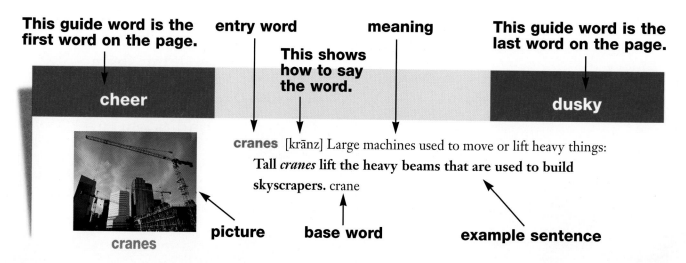

This guide word is the first word on the page.

entry word

meaning

This guide word is the last word on the page.

This shows how to say the word.

cheer

dusky

cranes [krānz] Large machines used to move or lift heavy things: **Tall *cranes* lift the heavy beams that are used to build skyscrapers.** crane

picture

base word

example sentence

cranes

A

a·lone [ə•lōn′] Away from everyone else; by oneself: **Matt was *alone* in the yard after the other children went into the house.**

a·long·side [ə•lông′sīd] Beside; at the side of: **Park your bike *alongside* the fence.**

an·gry [ang′grē] Upset: **I was *angry* with him for pushing me out of the way.**

an·nounced [ə•nounst′] Told others some news or information: **Our teacher *announced* to the class that we would have a special visitor.** announce, announcing

ar·rived [ə•rīvd′] Got to a place: **His plane *arrived* at the airport on time.** arrive, arriving

au·tumn [ô′təm] The time of year after summer and before winter: **The air gets cooler and leaves fall from the trees in *autumn*.** *syn.* fall

autumn

B

bat·ter [bat′ər] A mixture of flour, milk, eggs, and other things that will be made into a cake or pancakes: **Pour the cake *batter* into the pan and bake it.**

batter

beau·ti·ful [byo͞ot′i•fəl] Nice to look at: **The butterfly was so *beautiful* that I painted a picture of it.** *syns.* pretty, lovely

be·neath [bi•nēth′] Under: **We found the cat hiding *beneath* the sofa.**

but·ter·y [but′ə•rē] Having butter on it: **My fingers are *buttery* from the toast I just ate.**

beneath

365

chipmunks

cranes

cheer [chēr] To make someone who is unhappy feel better: **You can make a card to** *cheer* **a sick friend.** cheered, cheering

chip·munks [chip′mungks] Animals that look like small squirrels with stripes on their backs: **Two** *chipmunks* **ran under our porch.** chipmunk

chores [chôrz] Jobs that people do at home: **Setting the table and weeding the garden are two of my** *chores.* chore

clus·tered [klus′tərd] Got close together: **All the children** *clustered* **around the kitten.** cluster, clustering

com·plete·ly [kəm·plēt′lē] All the way; every bit: **The rain got us** *completely* **wet from head to foot.** complete

cranes [krānz] Large machines used to move or lift heavy things: **Tall** *cranes* **lift the heavy beams that are used to build skyscrapers.** crane

di·rec·tions [də·rek′shənz] Plans that tell how to do something or how to go somewhere: **Read the game's** *directions* **so you will know what to do.** *syn.* instructions

dull [dul] Not bright or shiny: **This bike was bright blue when it was new, but now its paint is** *dull.*

dusk·y [dus′kē] Half dark, as when night is coming: **We looked out the window at the** *dusky* **sky when we heard the storm was coming.**

en·gine [en′jən] The part of a car or other machine that causes it to move: **Dad opened the hood of the car so we could see the** *engine*.

e·nor·mous [i•nôr′məs] Very, very big: **The fish was so *enormous* that it wouldn't fit in the boat!** *syn.* huge

ex·cit·ing [ik•sīt′ing] Stirring up strong, lively feelings: **The movie was so *exciting* that we forgot to eat our popcorn.** *syn.* thrilling

ex·per·i·ment [ik•sper′ə•mənt] A test done to find out something: **We did an *experiment* to see if plants grow better near a window than in a dark closet.**

engine

fine [fīn] Good: **We had a *fine* time at the fair.**

fron·tier [frun•tir′] A place where people have not lived before: **Years ago, people moved to the *frontier* to find new land for homes and farms.**

frontier

gath·ered [ga<u>th</u>′ərd] Came together in a group: **The family *gathered* around Grandpa to listen to his story.** gather, gathering

glow·ing [glō′ing] Giving off a warm, soft light: **I love to watch the *glowing* fireflies on summer nights.**

grinned

glum [glum] Very unhappy: **Andy has been** *glum* **all day because his bike is missing.** *syns.* sad, gloomy

grand·daugh·ter [grand'dôt·ər] The daughter of a person's son or daughter: **The grandparents took care of their little** *granddaughter* **while her parents worked.**

grew [groo] Got bigger: **The little tree** *grew* **to be very tall.** grow, grown, growing

grinned [grind] Smiled a great big smile: **Maria was so glad to have a new puppy that she** *grinned* **all day.** grin, grinning

groups [groops] Sets of people or things: **Our class has four reading** *groups* **with six children in each group.** group

hand·some [han'səm] Good-looking: **A tiger has a** *handsome* **striped coat.**

hard·ly [härd'lē] Almost not: **He could** *hardly* **lift the heavy box.**

i·de·a [ī·dē'ə] A thought that a person has: **It was a good** *idea* **to put mittens on before playing in the snow.**

i·mag·ine [i·maj'in] Make a picture in one's mind; pretend: **Dan likes to** *imagine* **that his bed is a ship sailing on the sea.** imagined, imagining

knelt [nelt] Got down on one's knees: **He *knelt* down to pick up the pen he had dropped.** kneel, kneeling

knelt

loud [loud] Making a lot of sound; not quiet: **The jet made a *loud* noise that hurt my ears.** *syn.* noisy

mead·ow [med′ō] An open place where grass grows: **The cows ate grass in the *meadow*.**

mem·bers [mem′bərz] People who belong to a group such as a club or a team: **All the *members* of our reading group liked the story.** member

meadow

mo·tion [mō′shən] Movement: **The gentle *motion* of the rocking chair put the baby to sleep.**

near·by [nir•bī′] Not far; close by: **Mother stays *nearby* to watch us when we swim.**

nu·tri·tion [nōō•trish′ən] Feeding for health and growth: **Children need to eat many foods for good *nutrition*.**

369

orchard

photograph

pointed

or·chards [ôr′chərdz] Large groups of fruit trees or nut trees that people have planted: **Some farmers have planted** *orchards* **of apple, pear, and other fruit trees.** orchard

per·fect [pər′fikt] The best that something can be: **It was warm and sunny, a** *perfect* **day for a picnic.**

pho·to·graph [fō′tə·graf] A picture taken by a camera: **Look at this** *photograph* **my father took of me when I was a baby.**

picked [pikt] Took something such as a flower, a fruit, or a vegetable from a plant: **She** *picked* **a big bunch of flowers from her garden.** pick, picking

plant·ed [plant′əd] Put something into the ground so it would grow: **These flowers grew from the seeds we** *planted.* plant, planting

point·ed [point′əd] Used a finger to show someone something: **Juana** *pointed* **to the toy she wanted.** point, pointing

prom·ise [präm′əs] A statement that a person really will do something: **Don't make a** *promise* **if you are not sure you can keep it.**

pro·tects [prə·tekts′] Keeps safe: **Some animals have thick fur that** *protects* **them from the cold.** protect, protected, protecting

370

raced [rāst] Went very fast from one place to another: **Jenny *raced* home from school to tell her mother the good news.** race, racing

rea·son [rē′zən] A statement that tells why someone did something or why something happened: **The *reason* they are late is that the bus broke down.**

re·build [rē·bild′] To build again: **The farmer had to *rebuild* his barn after it burned down.** rebuilt, rebuilding

rec·i·pe [res′ə·pē] A plan that tells what items you need and what steps to follow to make something to eat or drink: **This *recipe* for popovers says to add two eggs.**

recipe

re·lay race [rē′lā rās] A race in which members of a team take turns running parts of the race: **In the *relay race*, each person on the team had to run to the tree and back.**

rip·ens [rī′pənz] Becomes fully grown, or ready to be used as food: **A tomato turns from green to red as it *ripens*.** ripen, ripened, ripening

relay race

shim·mered [shim′ərd] Shone with a soft sparkle: **The moonlight *shimmered* on the lake.** shimmer, shimmering

side·ways [sīd′wāz] To one side or the other: **I try to swim in a straight line, but I keep going *sideways*.**

sliver

sniffing

spins

sim·ple [sim′pəl] Easy to do or to understand: **Some math problems are hard, but this one is *simple*.**

sliv·er [sliv′ər] A very thin piece of something: **Dad was full after dinner, so he took only a tiny *sliver* of pie.**

smeared [smird] Spread something wet or greasy onto something else: **My little sister *smeared* finger paints all over the wall.** smear, smearing

sniff·ing [snif′ing] Breathing in through the nose in order to smell something: **Everyone kept *sniffing* the roses because they smelled so good.** sniff, sniffed

snug [snug] Warm and comfortable: **The children were *snug* in their warm beds that winter night.** *syn.* cozy

south [south] The direction to your right as you face the sunrise: **The plane turned and headed *south*.**

spar·kling [spär′kling] Shining in the light as a jewel does: **The dew on the grass was *sparkling* in the sunlight.** sparkle, sparkled *syn.* glittering

spins [spinz] Turns around and around: **The top *spins* more and more slowly until it falls over.** spin, spun, spinning *syn.* whirl

spoiled [spoild] Ruined; no longer useful: **The picture I drew was *spoiled* when I left it outside in the rain.** spoil, spoiling

spot·ted [spot′id] Saw something that might not be easy to see: **We *spotted* a plane flying high above.** spot, spotting

sprout [sprout] Begin to grow: **When the seeds *sprout*, tiny plants will push up through the ground.** sprouted, sprouting

stand [stand] A very small store or place outdoors for selling things: **The family grew vegetables and sold them at a *stand* by the road.**

streams [strēmz] Small rivers: **Fish live in ponds, lakes, rivers, *streams*, and oceans.** stream

strong [strông] Full of power; not weak: **The wind was so *strong* that it blew down some big trees.**

sur·prised [sər·prīzd′] Made someone feel as people do when something happens that they did not expect: **The loud bang *surprised* us and made us jump.** surprise, surprising

sur·vive [sər·vīv′] To stay alive: **Desert plants and animals can *survive* without much water.** survived, surviving

stand

tame [tām] To make something less wild: **You should not try to *tame* a wild animal by petting it.** tamed, taming

tool [tool] A thing you use to help you do work: **A drill is a *tool* that you can use to make holes in wood or metal.**

to·ward [tə·wôrd′] In the direction of: **I heard a splash, so I turned around and looked *toward* the lake.**

tur·nip [tûr′nip] A round vegetable that grows under the ground and may be white or yellow: **Mother cooked the *turnip* so we could eat it with our dinner.**

twitch [twich] To move quickly a part of the face or body: **I like to watch rabbits *twitch* their noses.** twitched, twitching

turnip

373

woods

wrinkled

yellow cake

wan·dered [wän′dərd] Walked as people do when they are not in a hurry: **We looked at bugs and smelled the flowers as we** *wandered* **across the field.** wander, wandering

which [hwich] The one that: **Her coat,** *which* **her mother had made for her, was red.**

wild [wīld] Not lived on or used by people: **Our country has made parks where no one may build so that the land will stay** *wild.*

won·der [wun′dər] To want to know: **I** *wonder* **who left this box here.** wondered, wondering

woods [woŏdz] A place where many trees grow: **Deer and other animals live in the** *woods.* *syn.* forest

wor·ry [wur′ē] To be upset by thinking about something that might happen: **When it doesn't rain, farmers** *worry* **that their crops will dry up.** worried, worrying

wrin·kled [ring′kəld] Became less smooth: **The clothes** *wrinkled* **in the hot dryer.** wrinkle, wrinkling

yel·low cake [yel′ō kāk] A kind of cake that is yellow in color: **Would you like a** *yellow cake* **or a chocolate cake for your birthday?**

374

Index *of*
Authors

Page numbers in color tell where you can read about the author.

Acknowledgments

For permission to reprint copyrighted material, grateful acknowledgment is made to the following sources:

Bayard Presse Canada Inc., Toronto, Canada: Adapted from "Fun Animal Facts," illustrated by Steve Attoe from *Chickadee* Magazine, April 1997. © 1997 by Owl Communications Corp.

Candlewick Press Inc., Cambridge, MA: Cover illustration by Jane Chapman from *One Duck Stuck* by Phyllis Root. Illustration copyright © 1998 by Jane Chapman.

Clarion Books/Houghton Mifflin Company: From *Helping Out* by George Ancona. Copyright © 1985 by George Ancona.

Dutton Children's Books, a division of Penguin Putnam Inc.: Cover illustration from *Way Out West Lives a Coyote Named Frank* by Jillian Lund. Illustration copyright © 1993 by Jillian Lund.

Greenwillow Books, a division of William Morrow & Company Inc.: Cover illustration by Lynn Sweat from *Amelia Bedelia Helps Out* by Peggy Parish. Illustration copyright © 1979 by Lynn Sweat. "Wind" and cover illustration from *Popcorn* by James Stevenson. Text and cover illustration copyright © 1998 by James Stevenson.

Harcourt, Inc.: Cover illustration from *Stellaluna* by Janell Cannon. Copyright © 1993 by Janell Cannon. "Pages" and cover illustration from *Bing Bang Boing* by Douglas Florian. Text and cover illustration copyright © 1994 by Douglas Florian. From *Mr. Putter and Tabby Fly the Plane* by Cynthia Rylant, illustrated by Arthur Howard. Text copyright © 1997 by Cynthia Rylant; illustrations copyright © 1997 by Arthur Howard. Cover illustration from *For Pete's Sake* by Ellen Stoll Walsh. Copyright © 1998 by Ellen Stoll Walsh.

HarperCollins Publishers: *What Makes Day and Night* by Franklyn M. Branley, cover illustration by Arthur Dorros. Text copyright © 1961, 1986 by Franklyn M. Branley; cover illustration copyright © 1986 by Arthur Dorros. *The Mixed-Up Chameleon* by Eric Carle. Copyright © 1975, 1984 in countries signatory to International Copyright Union. Cover illustration from *Feel the Wind* by Arthur Dorros. Copyright © 1989 by Arthur Dorros. From *Days With Frog and Toad* by Arnold Lobel. Copyright © 1979 by Arnold Lobel. *Lemonade for Sale* by Stuart J. Murphy, illustrated by Tricia Tusa. Text copyright © 1998 by Stuart J. Murphy; illustrations copyright © 1998 by Tricia Tusa. *When the Wind Stops* by Charlotte Zolotow, illustrated by Stefano Vitale. Text copyright © 1962, 1995 by Charlotte Zolotow; illustrations copyright © 1995 by Stefano Vitale.

Holiday House, Inc.: *From Seed to Plant* by Gail Gibbons. Copyright © 1991 by Gail Gibbons. Cover illustration from *Who's Who in My Family?* by Loreen Leedy. Copyright © 1995 by Loreen Leedy.

Henry Holt and Company, Inc.: *Watermelon Day* by Kathi Appelt, illustrated by Dale Gottlieb. Text copyright © 1996 by Kathi Appelt; illustrations copyright © 1996 by Dale Gottlieb.

Pyke Johnson, Jr.: "Lemonade" by Pyke Johnson, Jr.

Little Brown and Company: From *All Join In* by Quentin Blake. Copyright © 1990 by Quentin Blake. "Sometimes" from *Fathers, Mothers, Sisters, Brothers* by Mary Ann Hoberman, cover illustration by Marylin Hafner.

Text copyright © 1991 by Mary Ann Hoberman; cover illustration copyright © 1991 by Marylin Hafner.

Lothrop, Lee & Shepard Books, a division of William Morrow & Company, Inc.: Cover photograph by Ken Heyman from *Puddle Jumper; How a Toy Is Made* by Ann Morris. Photograph copyright © 1993 by Ken Heyman.

Orchard Books, New York: Cover illustration by Patricia Mullins from *Shoes from Grandpa* by Mem Fox. Illustration copyright © 1989 by Patricia Mullins. Cover illustration by Nancy Poydar from *Beezy at Bat* by Megan McDonald. Illustration copyright © 1998 by Nancy Poydar.

G. P. Putnam's Sons, a division of Penguin Putnam Inc.: Cover illustration by Kathleen Kuchera from *The Rooster Who Went to His Uncle's Wedding* by Alma Flor Ada. Illustration copyright © 1993 by Kathleen Kuchera.

Random House Children's Books, a division of Random House, Inc., New York, NY: *Hedgehog Bakes a Cake* by Maryann Macdonald, illustrated by Lynn Munsinger. Copyright © 1990 by Byron Preiss Visual Publications, Inc. Text copyright © 1990 by Maryann Macdonald; illustrations copyright © 1990 by Lynn Munsinger. Cover illustration from *Somewhere in the World Right Now* by Stacey Schuett. Copyright © 1995 by Stacey Schuett.

Scholastic, Inc.: Cover illustration from *Ruby the Copycat* by Peggy Rathmann. Copyright © 1991 by Margaret Rathmann.

Simon & Schuster Books for Young Readers, Simon & Schuster Children's Publishing Division: *Wilson Sat Alone* by Debra Hess, illustrated by Diane Greenseid. Text copyright © 1994 by Debra Hess; illustrations copyright © 1994 by Diane Greenseid. From *Henry and Mudge Under the Yellow Moon* by Cynthia Rylant, illustrated by Suçie Stevenson. Text copyright © 1987 by Cynthia Rylant; illustrations copyright © 1987 by Suçie Stevenson. Cover illustration by Mary Szilagyi from *This Year's Garden* by Cynthia Rylant. Illustration copyright © 1984 by Mary Szilagyi. Cover illustration from *Flowers, Fruits, Seeds* by Jerome Wexler. Copyright © 1987 by Jerome Wexler.

Photo Credits

Key: (t)=top, (b)=bottom, (c)=center, (l)=left, (r)=right
Carlo Ontal, 44; Ian Anderson, 65; courtesy, Eric Carle, 125; Stephen Dalton/NHPA, 126-127; Carolyn A. McKeone/Photo Researchers, 151(l); Chris Jones/The Stock Market, 151(c); Superstock, 151(r); George Ancona, 154-167, 170-171; Carlo Ontal, 194; Dominic Oldershaw, 271(l); courtesy, Gail Gibbons, 291; courtesy, Kathi Appelt, 317(l); courtesy, Franklyn M. Branley, 357(t); G. Ryan & S. Beyer/Tony Stone Images, 364; Bruce Barthei/The Stock Market, 365; Tom McHugh/Photo Researchers, 366(t); G. Ryan & S. Beyer/Tony Stone Images, 366(b); Paul Chauncey/The Stock Market, 367(t); Indiana Historical Society Library, 367(b); Myrleen Cate/Tony Stone Images, 368; Oddo Sinibaldi/The Stock Market, 369(b); Dick Thomas/Visual Unlimited, 370(t); Peter Cade/Tony Stone Images, 372(b); John Paul Endress/The Stock Market, 373(t); Terry Donnelly/Tom Stack & Associates, 374(t).
All other photos by Harcourt:
Kevin Delanhunty/Black Star, Chuck Kneyse/Black Star, Rick Friedman/Black Star, Lisa Quiñones/Black Star, Todd Bigelow/Black Star, Walt Chrynwski/Black Star, David Levensen/Black Star, Larry Evans/Black Star, Janice Rubin/Black Star, Rick Falco/Black Star, Kevin Miller/Black Star, Ken Kenzie, Maria Paraskevas, Dale Higgins.

Illustration Credits

Steve Johnson/Lou Fancher, Cover Art; Tom Casmer, 2-3, 10-11, 12-13, 130-131; Jennie Oppenheimer, 4-5, 132-133, 134-135, 246-247; Donna Perrone, 6-7, 248-249, 250-251, 362-363; Lisa Campbell Ernst, 14-29, 32-33; Holly Cooper, 30-31, 365, 371, 372; Suçie Stevenson, 34-45, 46-47; Katy Farmer, 48-49; Arnold Lobel, 50-65, 68-69; Steve Johnson, 66-67; Diane Greenseid, 70-89, 90-91; Tuko Fujisaki, 92-93, 320-321; Eric Carle, 94-125, 128-129; Scott Goto, 136-149, 150-151; Billy Davis, 152-153; George Ancona, 154-167, 170-171; Quentin Blake, 168-169; Arthur Howard, 172-195, 196-197; Lynn Munsinger, 198-217, 218-219; David Herrick, 220-221; Tricia Tusa, 222-241, 244-245; Jennifer Beck-Harris, 242-243; Victoria Raymond, 252-271, 272-273; Gail Gibbons, 274-291, 292-293, 294-295; Dale Gottlieb, 296-317, 318-319; Stefano Vitale, 322-341, 344-345; Doug Bowles, 342-343; D. R. Greenlaw, 346-357, 358-359; David Herrick, 360-361